D1452002

# Feudal Architecture
of Japan

# Volume 13

## THE HEIBONSHA SURVEY OF JAPANESE ART

*For a list of the entire series see end of book*

### CONSULTING EDITORS

Katsuichiro Kamei, *art critic*
Seiichiro Takahashi, *Chairman, Japan Art Academy*
Ichimatsu Tanaka, *Chairman, Cultural Properties Protection Commission*

# Feudal Architecture of Japan

*by* KIYOSHI HIRAI

translated by Hiroaki Sato
and Jeannine Ciliotta

New York · WEATHERHILL / HEIBONSHA · Tokyo

This book was originally published in Japanese by Heibonsha
under the title *Shiro to Shoin* in the Nihon no Bijutsu series.

*First English Edition, 1973*
*Second Printing, 1980*

*Jointly published by John Weatherhill, Inc., of New York and Tokyo, with edito-
rial offices at 7–6–13, Roppongi, Minato-ku, Tokyo 106, and Heibonsha, Tokyo.
Copyright © 1965, 1973, by Heibonsha; all rights reserved. Printed in Japan.*

*Library of Congress Cataloging in Publication Data:* Hirai, Kiyoshi, 1929– /
Feudal architecture of Japan. / (The Heibonsha survey of Japanese Art) /
Translation of Shiro to shoin. / 1. Castles—Japan. 2. Architecture, Shoin.
I. Title. II. Series. / NA7451.H4813 / 728.8′1′0952 / 73-3354 / ISBN
0-8348-1015-8

# Contents

# Feudal Architecture
## of Japan

CHAPTER ONE

# The Castle

DEVELOPMENT OF THE CASTLE   The surrounding of an area with defensive structures developed in conjunction with strife among peoples. At first, embankments, stone fences, wooden fences, and moats were used as fortifications. In one picture scroll depicting thirteenth- and fourteenth-century residences in Japan, rural manor houses had the simplest of fortifications—wooden palisades along moats and wooden towers above gates—chiefly because wars were still being fought with primitive weapons, such as bows and arrows, spears, and swords. A scene from this scroll (Fig. 2) depicts a local lord's residence fortified with a moat and a protective structure built on the front gate, but it is far from what we normally call a castle.

During the Nara period (646–794) the Dazaifu, or Kyushu Defense Headquarters, located a few miles inland from Hakata Bay in northern Kyushu, constructed a *mizuki* (literally, "water fort"), a damlike embankment, so that the area could be flooded to make an artificial lake in time of war. This bulwark, the remnants of which still exist, was built between the Dazaifu and Hakata Bay as protection against invasions from the Korean peninsula. The words *kinowa* and *kinowasaku,* also containing the character *ki*, "castle," refer to a fort surrounded by a wall with turrets. These forts were built by the frontier guards sent to northern Japan during the eighth century to suppress the aboriginal inhabitants of the region, who were in active rebellion against the central government. A *kinowa* has been excavated in Yamagata Prefecture.

Sometime after the Nara period the character *ki* came to be pronounced *shiro*, as it still is today; according to one theory this change occurred in the Heian period (794–1185). The only importance this has for us here is to make it clear that *ki* and *shiro* (or *jiro* in combined words) are the same character, meaning castle, and that in the following discussion we are still dealing with the same fortress-castle concept, even though the pronunciation of the word has changed.

The Onin Civil War (1467–77), which was fought in and around Kyoto, weakened the Muromachi military government established in Kyoto by the Ashikaga clan (the family of shoguns who ruled from 1336 to 1573). The local warriors grew more powerful, and many fortresses were built during the latter part of the sixteenth century. As guns were introduced and war tactics became more sophisticated, fortresses were made larger in scale and more complicated in defensive structures.

Fortresses were usually built atop steep mountains. At first a flat-topped mountain or an area near the top of a mountain that could be leveled was chosen as a castle site (Fig. 1). Stone walls (Fig. 3) were raised around these structures, and toward the end of Japan's middle ages, that is, toward the end of the sixteenth century, small donjons, or towers, were added. Buttressed by its natural setting, and making the best possible use of

*1. Mount Gagyu, the site of Bitchu-Matsuyama Castle, and the castle town. Bitchu, Okayama Prefecture.*

the surrounding topography, this *yamajiro,* as the mountain castle (Fig. 13) was called, was extremely difficult to attack directly. Siege was the only effective strategy that could be used against it. Castles and donjons located on mountaintops, therefore, had to have additional permanent structures, such as residential quarters and warehouses for storing food and weapons against a long siege. As further preparation against possible siege, the donjon itself often had a well and a kitchen.

Since the environment at the top of a mountain was convenient neither for maintaining troops nor for daily living, residences for the daimyo, or feudal lord, and individual quarters for soldiers were built at the foot of the mountain. A *jokamachi,* or castle town (Fig. 1), developed as these buildings were surrounded by the houses of merchants and arti-

sans. Since the site for a *yamajiro* was chosen for strategic reasons, the castle was not easily accessible, and frequently the immediate surroundings were unfit for the development of a town. Therefore, later castles, *hirayamajiro,* came to be built on a hill in the middle of a plain in the heart of a daimyo's territory.

The daimyos who survived the Age of the Warring Provinces (1482–1558) and succeeded in expanding their territories built larger castles as their spheres of influence increased. As wars occurred less frequently the castle not only became more dignified but also was regarded as a political center from which to rule territory rather than as a strategically located military base. Long before peace came to the land, the Japanese castle was meant less as a fort than as a symbol of power. The castle

2. *Fortifications of a rural manor house as depicted in a fourteenth-century picture scroll.*

3. *Remains of main gate of Bitchu-Matsuyama Castle. 1681–84. Bitchu, Okayama Prefecture.*

was built in an open area, wherever the political and economic life of a territory was concentrated; and a donjon soaring majestically from the center of the castle compound was an effective symbol of the leader's authority. Defensive aspects, however, were not neglected. Sites were chosen where lakes, rivers, or seas could be utilized as moats; and extensive stone walls were put up around the castle compound. This flatland castle is called a *hirajiro*, and examples include Nagoya Castle and Nijo Castle (Figs. 7, 112) in Kyoto. These two castles were constructed early in the seventeenth century exclusively to display the power and authority of their residents and were never exposed to attack during the Edo period (1603–1868).

The Japanese castle differed basically from the castles of Europe and China. In Europe, some castles were built independently as forts away from cities; but since most castles were built in cities, walls were put up around the cities to protect the citizens from battles. Similarly, in China walls were erected around cities or at borders against invading forces—for example, the Great Wall of China. In contrast, Japan has seldom been invaded by other countries, and its civil wars involved only warriors, rarely peasants or merchants. As a consequence, the town surrounding a castle was seldom regarded as part of the fort. In most instances fortifications were concentrated at the castle, the daimyo's headquarters. Its donjon, the central tower of the castle, was his final refuge.

As a rule, the warrior did not plan to fight from within the castle—rather, he regarded fighting outside the castle as the best defense. Therefore, in

4. *Drawing of Hideyoshi's Juraku-dai castle-palace. (See also Figure 40.)*

building a castle, he fortified the borders of his compound; and when his castle was besieged he made it a rule and a point of honor to go out to the battlefield. Since he had no weaponry with which to assail the castle effectively, the invader usually avoided direct attack and resorted to siege; and when a siege was expected to last for months he sometimes built his own castle nearby.

The military dictator Toyotomi Hideyoshi* (1536–98) is known for having employed this tactic on a grand scale. In attacking one of the vassals of Mori Terumoto (1553–1625), a powerful daimyo in western Honshu, at Bitchu-Takamatsu Castle in present-day Okayama Prefecture, Hideyoshi obstructed the flow of the Ashimori River

* The names of all premodern Japanese in this book are given, as in this case, in Japanese style (surname first); those of all modern (post-1868) Japanese are given in Western style (surname last).

with an embankment two kilometers long and isolated the castle in an artificial lake. He attacked the daimyos Hojo Ujimasa (1538–90) and Hojo Ujinao (1562–91) at Odawara in 1590 for failing to comply with certain of his requests; by building a castle virtually overnight on Ishigaki Mountain and waiting until the Hojo food supply was exhausted, he was able to defeat them. In an age when protracted siege was the general rule, the castle was less a defensive fortress than a symbol of defensive capability with which to impress or discourage the enemy.

Chronicles of the Age of the Warring Provinces record few battles as ever having reached the donjon. The daimyos were unwilling to fight enemy troops who successfully broke into their castle grounds; as soon as it became apparent that the battle was going against them, they more frequently than not chose to die an honorable death

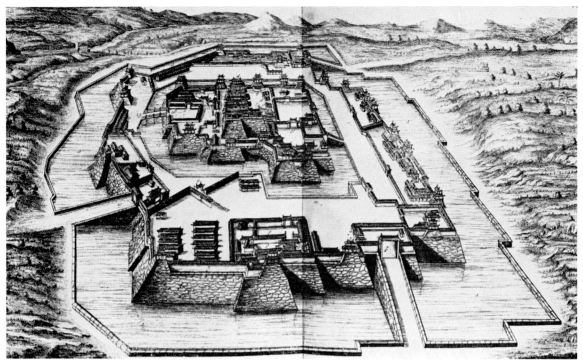

5. *Tokugawa Ieyasu's Osaka Castle as depicted by the Dutch missionary Montanus in his book,* Nihon Shi *(Chronicle of Japan).*
*Seventeenth century.*

at their own hands. The donjon, a good place from which to observe enemy movements and command the battle, was also where a defender could commit ritual suicide if defense ended unsuccessfully. When his castle fell, the defeated daimyo was prepared to die gallantly, and in many instances he destroyed the donjon, the symbol of his power, as well as himself. According to *An Account of the Shizugatake Battle of 1583,* Shibata Katsuie (1530–83), a daimyo, had a mass of straw set afire on the first floor of his donjon. The straw had been stored there for use on just such an occasion. When the entire donjon was wrapped in flames the daimyo, on the fifth floor, faced his enemy's camp and committed suicide.

The major consideration in castle building was to arrange the buildings on the chosen site in such a way as to make the complex formidable to an attacker. The main compound (the *hommaru* com-

pound), containing the donjon and the daimyo's residential quarters, was the heart of the castle complex; and subsidiary compounds were added as the complex expanded. Stone walls and moats were placed concentrically or spirally around the main and subsidiary compounds of the castle complex, completely surrounding them (see foldout following page 36). Turrets were built on the walls, the largest of them located at strategic corners.

Attempts had been made to strengthen the walls of the buildings by adding layers of plaster to them, but because these wooden structures were still vulnerable, the strong fortified outworks were also necessary. The walls, made of stones that had not been shaped in any way, were steep, and wall-scalers could not gain an easy foothold. But maze-like inner areas were still necessary to obstruct the enemy's attempts at storming the main compound. Against just such an attack, the path approaching

6. *Donjon of Edo Castle before the Meireki fire in 1657, as depicted in the* Tokaido Emaki *(Picture Scroll of the Tokaido). Tokyo University.*

the main compound had many twists and took un-expected turns in the opposite direction. Upon turning these corners, the enemy would be stopped by gates and fired upon from the interstices in the walls surrounding the path and from the turrets above.

Outside the moat immediately surrounding the castle was the castle town, with the houses of the warriors (from top-ranking head retainers to foot soldiers), merchants, and artisans. A town's general boundaries were frequently determined by topography and by the roads running nearby, but the sections within the town were laid out in a checker-board pattern. As a precaution against attacks by outsiders, a number of blind alleys were deliberately built, and some streets were blocked in many unexpected spots to prevent a clear view of just where they led.

The higher a warrior's rank, the closer to the castle he was allowed to live. Often as an extra line of defense there was an outer moat around this district where high-ranking warriors lived, separating it from the rest of the town. Such an arrangement can be seen in the site plan for Himeji Castle (Fig. 31). During the early part of the Edo period, for reasons of administrative efficiency, town residents were made to live in areas segregated according to their occupations. However, as the economic position of the warrior class deteriorated, this practice could not be enforced.

DONJONS  Although Tokugawa Ieyasu (1542–1616) became the undisputed ruler of Japan after winning the Battle of Sekigahara in 1600, the times were still turbulent, and major battles threatened to break out at any moment. In

*7. Aerial view of stone foundation of Nijo Castle donjon in Hommaru Compound. 1626. Kyoto. (See also Figure 112.)*

order to deal with this situation, Ieyasu placed reliable hereditary daimyos, and those who had contributed to his victory, in strategic areas. This meant a broad redistribution of the daimyos. As a result, many new castles were built after the Battle of Sekigahara. Moreover, these lords had to build castles excelling in size, beauty, and dignity the ones previously held by the vanquished daimyos. Thus castle construction was at its peak at this time.

As an architectural means of displaying samurai superiority, impressive interiors had been fully developed in the *shoin* structures, which are discussed later. But these were seen only by people of the upper strata—the peerage, military men of high rank, and wealthy merchants. The conquering daimyos had to display their power and authority to all the people they ruled—and for that purpose

the donjon was most effective. Consequently, of all the castle structures exposed to the view of commoners, the donjon, being the tallest tower and therefore the most conspicuous part of the castle, was covered with brilliant white plaster, giving the castle a resplendent appearance.

The multistoried donjon is thought to have originated in the practice of building a watchtower atop a manor-house roof. Examples of the earliest donjons include the donjon of Maruoka Castle (Figs. 19, 20), Fukui Prefecture, the oldest extant *hirayamajiro*; and the donjon of Inuyama Castle (Figs. 11, 55), Aichi Prefecture. The donjons of Okayama, Kumamoto, and Himeji castles are examples of donjons at the height of their development. The donjon of Okayama Castle (Figs. 8, 21) had two two-story turrets (one atop the other), on top of which was a watchtower. Large gables pro-

*8. Donjon of Okayama Castle in Okayama Prefecture. Completed, 1597; destroyed by bombing, 1945. (See also Figure 21.)*

ject into the eaves of the uppermost story of the donjons of Himeji (Figs. 9, 10) and Kumamoto (Figs. 14, 51) castles. These gables are vestiges of the large roofs of the two-story turrets on earlier castles. Large gables like these not only were hard to set in place, but the junctures where gables and roofs met were not well suited for permitting rainwater to be carried off. Later, a gabled roof composed of two small gables, which could be set under the upper roof, was devised.

Because of the limited space on mountaintops and the problems of building on steep slopes, a massive rectangular stone base had to be built as the foundation for a castle. Although foundation excavation and reclamation work was done, it was technically difficult during the 1600s to build square stone foundations. Therefore, because the floors and walls of the first and upper stories were

not always parallel, hipped-and-gabled roofs were necessary for making various structural adjustments. When advanced techniques of stonework made possible an even foundation regardless of the topography, it also became possible, as the donjon rose, to reduce the floor spaces systematically and place the ridges of the roof at the corners of the uppermost floor. As a result, the gable, which had been structurally indispensable in roof building, now became superfluous, and the donjon of Tsuyama Castle (Fig. 23), Okayama Prefecture, and the original donjon of Kokura Castle, Fukuoka Prefecture, have no gables, although the rebuilt Kokura Castle donjon does have gables. But even after the gable became technically unnecessary, in most castles it continued to be used as an ornament.

Two kinds of gables were commonly used: the sharply triangular dormer gable, and the *karahafu*,

9. Main donjon of Himeji Castle, with northwest (far left) and west small donjons. Completed 1609. Himeji, Hyogo Prefecture. (See also Figures 10, 27, 30.)

10 (overleaf). Northwest (left) and west (right) small donjons of Himeji Castle seen from below, ▷ with main donjon rising behind them. Completed 1609. Himeji, Hyogo Prefecture. (See also Figures 9, 27, 30.)

12. *Donjon of Iyo-Matsuyama Castle. 1854. Matsuyama, Ehime Prefecture. (See also Figure 61.)*

◁ 11. *Donjon of Inuyama Castle, with fortified entrance. 1600. Inuyama, Aichi Prefecture. (See also Figures 55, 56.)*

14. *Main turret of Kumamoto Castle. 1607. Kumamoto City, Kumamoto Prefecture. (See also Figure 51.)*

◁  13. *Donjon of Bitchu-Matsuyama Castle. 1683. Bitchu, Okayama Prefecture.*

*15. Donjon of Hirosaki Castle.*
*1810. Hirosaki, Aomori Prefecture.*

17. *Earthen-walled inner moat of Edo Castle. Seventeenth century. Tokyo. (See also Figures 47, 48.)*

◁  16. *Fortified Ishikawa Gate of Kanazawa Castle. 1788. Kanazawa, Ishikawa Prefecture. (See also Figure 52.)*

19. *Donjon of Maruoka Castle, the oldest complete extant* hirayamajiro. *1576. Maruoka, Fukui Prefecture. (See also Figures 20, 24, 53.)*

a Chinese-style gable that had undulating barge-boards with a flattened central arch and trailing ends. The donjon of Maruoka Castle (Figs. 19, 20, 53) has dormer-style gables on the roofs of the first story, and that of Inuyama Castle (Fig. 11) has *karahafu* gables. Sometimes gables were built over structures added to strengthen the defense of the donjon. For example, the dormer-style gables on the first level of the donjon of Nagoya Castle (Fig. 22) were atop small boxlike projections called *ishi otoshi*, which had trapdoors from which stones could be dropped on enemy forces trying to climb the walls. But most later gables covered no such practical structures. The gables of the donjon of Hirosaki Castle (Fig. 15), Aomori Prefecture, are typical. Here several gables serving a purely deco-

rative function were built on the front side of the donjon, but none was built on the side facing the castle compound.

Smaller, two- or three-story turrets, also built for defense purposes and strategically located at important parts of the castle, were of essentially the same construction as the donjon. The gate of the castle was made of two leaves of wood covered with iron, and heavily fortified (Fig. 16). Often the turret above the gate contained apertures from which stones could be hurled. These entrance fortifications were necessary because the first donjons, which were built during the Muromachi period (1336–1568), were constructed apart from the other buildings and were therefore very vulnerable.

In the donjon of Azuchi Castle, Shiga Prefecture,

◁ *18. Himeji Castle I Gate and turret seen across Sangoku Moat. Completed 1609. Himeji, Hyogo Prefecture.*

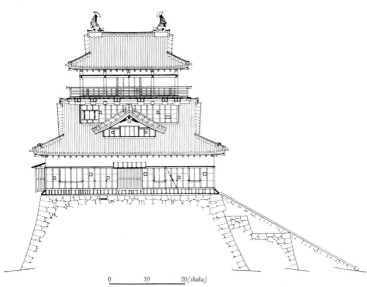

20. *Elevation of donjon of Maruoka Castle completed in 1576. (See also Figures 19, 24, 53.)*

0    10    20*(shaku)*

a small passage cut through one of the surrounding stone walls was used for entering the donjon. And Maruoka Castle had a staircase built on one side (Fig. 24), which led directly to the first level of the tower. Because these entryways could be attacked so easily, various defensive structures were devised to ward off an approaching enemy. In Inuyama Castle, a turret was built beside the entrance of the donjon, and this attached turret was further developed in Matsue Castle (Figs. 25, 58), Shimane Prefecture, so that entry had to be gained through the turret. The donjon of Matsumoto Castle (Figs. 26, 42), Nagano Prefecture, was further strengthened with a small donjon and a turret, and its entrance is built beneath the fortified corridor that connects the small donjon to the main donjon.

In Nagoya Castle, a different type of entrance plan was devised. To reach the donjon one first had to enter the small donjon and then pass through a roofless corridor between two high fences. The most elaborate defense structures ever devised for a donjon are found in Himeji (Figs. 27, 30), Hyogo

Prefecture, and Iyo-Matsuyama, Ehime Prefecture, castles, where the donjon is connected to three smaller donjons by covered corridors. In order to reach the donjon, an enemy force had to pass through the entrance gate beneath one of the corridors, then go through a small court in which it was exposed to attack from all four donjons. These four towers, soaring into the sky, were effective not only for defense but also for the display of power.

Death, always imminent for the warrior, was one of his main concerns. Thus the top floor of a donjon often included residential quarters appropriate for his last moments. The donjon of Okayama Castle, built in the period 1594–97 (or, according to another theory, in 1589), had residential quarters on the second floor equipped with the decorative elements of a formal reception room—a tokonoma, *chigaidana* (the adjoining ornamental shelves used for displaying treasured objects), and *chodaigamae* (the ornately decorated sliding doors that opened onto a sleeping alcove).

A small donjon built in Kumamoto Castle in 1608 had residential quarters decorated with a

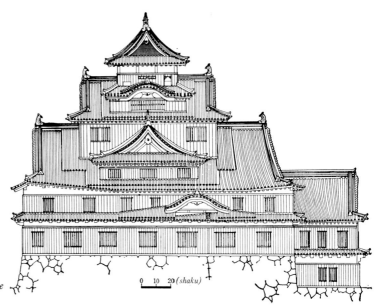

21. Elevation of donjon of Okayama Castle completed in 1597. (See also Figure 8.)

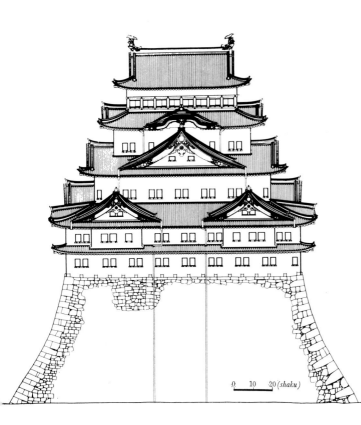

22. Elevation of donjon of Nagoya Castle completed in 1612.

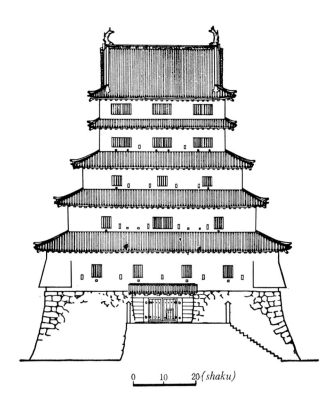

23. *Elevation of donjon of Tsuyama Castle as reconstructed by Dr. Michio Fujioka.*

0    10    20 *(shaku)*

tokonoma and a *tsukeshoin* (an alcove containing a large window with a broad sill about one-third of a meter above the floor). Since the castle also had a reception hall with all the usual formal decorative elements, the donjon was probably not intended for receiving guests. Although Kato Kiyomasa (1562–1611), lord of the castle, had sided with Tokugawa Ieyasu in the Battle of Sekigahara, he was nonetheless loyal to the Toyotomi family, rivals of the Tokugawas. Perhaps he prepared the reception room for Hideyori, the young heir of the Toyotomi family. It is hard to imagine anyone wanting to live in the donjon: it was a military structure intended for use in an emergency, such as a siege, and no effort had been made to make it a comfortable place in which to live. Furthermore, residential quarters were located in the many other buildings near the donjon.

CASTLES AND DONJONS  The donjon is the central architectural feature of the castle; and the earliest modern donjon was that of Azuchi Castle, built in 1576 by the powerful warlord Oda Nobunaga (1534–82). The castle, constructed on a small hill (Fig. 29) in Omi Province (present-day Shiga Prefecture), was burned soon after Nobunaga's death; and the only reminders of its glorious past are a few remnants of the foundation stones (Fig. 28). The castle was a mixture of fort and residence, and its six-story donjon was the first to be constructed for the purpose of displaying the power of a warrior. The exterior walls were decorated with colored plaster, and all the rooms contained paintings by the famous artist Kano Eitoku (1543–90). Today, rice paddies surround the foot of the hill where once there was a lake, and nothing resembling the

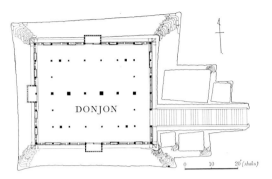

24. *Ground plan of donjon of Maruoka Castle completed in 1576. (See also Figures 19, 20, 53.)*

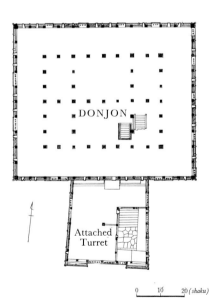

25. *Ground plan of donjon of Matsue Castle completed in 1611. (See also Figure 58.)*

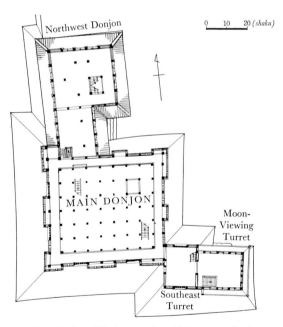

26. *Ground plan of donjon complex of Matsumoto Castle completed in 1598. (See also Figures 42, 43.)*

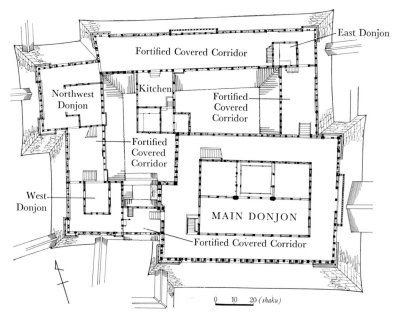

*27. Ground plan of donjon complex of Himeji Castle completed in 1609. (See also Figures 9, 30.)*

bustling castle town remains. But in Nobunaga's day, this strategically located town connected Kyoto with the Hokuriku (central Japan Sea coast of Honshu) district and the Mino area (present-day Gifu Prefecture), and the six-story donjon presented an impressive sight to the people who passed through the town in large numbers.

At the base of Azuchi's donjon there remain foundation stones indicative of a storage cellar. These foundation stones, set seven *shaku*, or more than two meters,* apart, suggest the immense size of the donjon. According to Ota Gyuichi's *Nobu-*

---

*\* Japanese architecture is based on a grid plan with a fundamental measurement of one *ken* and a supplemental unit of half a *ken*. The *ken* itself is a variable unit; for example, the mid-sixteenth-century *ken* was usually equal to seven *shaku* (a bit more than two meters). Following that, in warriors' and noblemen's houses one *ken* was six and a half *shaku*; for commoners it was six *shaku*.*

*naga's Life,* completed in 1587, the donjon, 33 meters high, 35.7 meters from east to west, and 42.4 meters from north to south, rose six stories from the base. The height of the donjon slightly exceeds the height of the Himeji Castle donjon. Luis Frois (c.1532–97), a Portuguese Jesuit missionary, reported that the tower's outer walls were painted scarlet, blue, and gold—a different color for each story—and the window frames were lacquered black. Nobunaga, who liked to be first, was proud of the unprecedented structure he had created.

At that time, the methods used for building donjons were still primitive. If large-scale donjons were to be built, the basic structure—a fort with a watchtower placed on the roof, as exemplified by the donjon of Maruoka Castle (Fig. 53)—had either to be enlarged or to have additional stories added to it. Simply increasing the size of the donjon

*28. Remains of foundation of donjon of Azuchi Castle. Sixteenth century. Azuchi, Shiga Prefecture.*

resulted in a discrepancy between the outer appearance and the interior structure. The donjon of Kochi Castle (Fig. 63), built in 1747, for instance, looks like a three-story structure from the outside but actually has six floors inside.

However, at the time that Azuchi Castle was built, this inconsistent method of construction was not yet in widespread use. The donjon of Azuchi Castle consisted of a two-story base fort upon which another two-story fort was built, and upon this there was a two-story watchtower. An attic was added, making the donjon a six-story, seven-floor building. The general appearance of this donjon could be surmised until recently from the donjon of Okayama Castle (Fig. 8), which is thought to have been built in imitation of it. The donjon of Okayama Castle had a base fort with hipped-and-gabled roofs upon which was built a small fort with a watchtower above. Unfortunately, Okayama

Castle was destroyed during an air raid in 1945.

The donjon of Azuchi Castle, of impressive size and casting a colorful reflection on Lake Biwa, differed from other rough military structures in yet another respect—it had numerous reception rooms. According to "In the Donjon of Mount Azuchi" in *Nobunaga's Life,* on the floor immediately above the stone foundation there was a room with a mural depicting plum trees painted in ink on a gold ground on the *fusuma* (opaque sliding partitions between rooms). Another room had a mural depicting Chinese Confucian scholars, and many other chambers were just as resplendent. It was here that Nobunaga entertained the tea masters of Sakai (a commercial port city south of Osaka). Nevertheless, the reception rooms in the donjon were structurally restricted in size. Since the largest rooms in the Azuchi donjon contained only twelve tatami mats (each of which measured roughly one

29. *Azuchi Mountain, the site of Azuchi Castle. Azuchi, Shiga Prefecture.*

meter by two meters), larger and more impressive rooms were built in the more spacious buildings of the main compound.

Near the donjon, in a style no less attractive, was the Hommaru Palace, that is, the palace in the *hommaru* (main) compound, Nobunaga's own residential quarters. According to a passage in *Nobunaga's Life* concerning New Year's Day, 1582, Nobunaga showed the palace to nobles from various areas. The Room of the Imperial Visit had fixed partitions (instead of *fusuma*) inlaid with gold, all its metalwork was of gold gilt, and the ceiling had a latticed pattern. By displaying golden murals and other splendid decorations that generously adorned the donjon and the palace, Nobunaga undoubtedly tried to show that his castle was far superior to the castles of the other lords, whose donjons indeed looked rude in comparison. When he entertained foreign missionaries, he not only guided them around the castle but presented them with a pair of screens depicting the castle and the surrounding town. In giving the screens, he hoped that his castle in all its glory would be known in distant foreign lands. Unfortunately, all these screens were taken out of Japan, and their locations, as well as the exact appearance of the castle, remain unknown.

The military dictator Toyotomi Hideyoshi built

30. *Aerial view of donjon complex of Himeji Castle. In left foreground, in front of and connected to main donjon, is east donjon, which is connected by fortified corridor to northwest donjon (right foreground), which is connected by another fortified corridor to west donjon (right background); roof of kitchen is just visible in courtyard bounded by the fortified corridors. Completed 1609. Himeji, Hyogo Prefecture. (See also Figures 9, 27.)*

Osaka Castle in 1582, and he ruled Japan from there until his death. Osaka Castle was almost completely destroyed during the Sieges of Osaka Castle (1614–15); and Tokugawa Ieyasu, emerging victorious from these wars, had the daimyos rebuild the castle from completely different plans. Nothing of Hideyoshi's castle remains today. The oldest extant turret of the castle is that built in 1626 by the Tokugawas: the donjon built in 1626 was destroyed by lightning in 1665. The present donjon (Fig. 38) was rebuilt on the foundation of the Tokugawa castle and resembles Hideyoshi's donjon.

Hideyoshi, who had a great interest in architecture, built one large-scale castle after another:

Himeji Castle in 1581, Osaka Castle in 1582, and the Juraku-dai castle-palace in 1587; in 1589 he began Yodo Castle in the Kyoto area; in 1592, Nagoya Castle in northern Kyushu, near present-day Karatsu; and in 1594, Fushimi Castle in Kyoto. To build these castles, we know that he requisitioned materials and labor from the daimyos he ruled; but most of these castles are not extant and further information on them is not available.

The present Himeji Castle (Fig. 9), located in Himeji, Hogo Prefecture, was built after the Battle of Sekigahara. Because Himeji was one of the strategic areas on the way to the western provinces, castles had been built there as early as the Age of

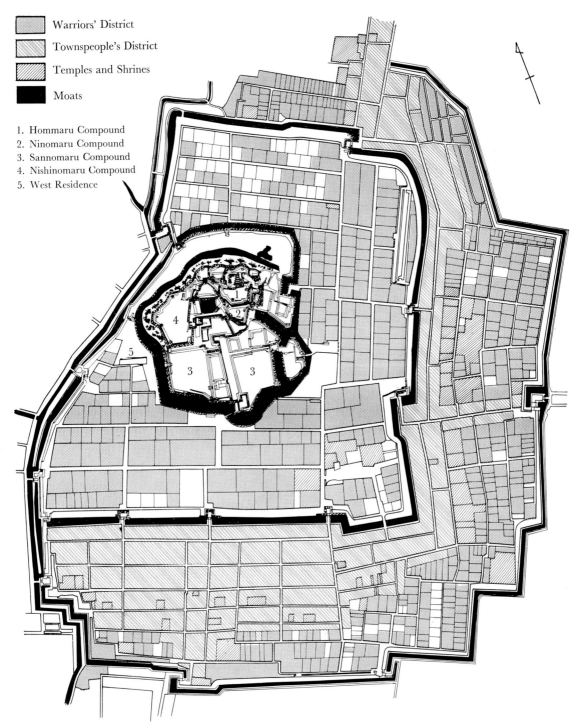

Warriors' District

Townspeople's District

Temples and Shrines

Moats

1. Hommaru Compound
2. Ninomaru Compound
3. Sannomaru Compound
4. Nishinomaru Compound
5. West Residence

*31. Ground plan of Himeji Castle and surrounding castle town about 1750.*

32. *Himeji Castle. Completed 1609. Himeji, Hyogo Prefecture.*

the Northern and Southern Courts (1336–92), when the imperial court was split into two factions, one at Kyoto and the other at Yoshino, in present-day Nara Prefecture. In order to subdue the daimyos of the provinces in western Japan, Toyotomi Hideyoshi, commanding Oda Nobunaga's forces, invaded this area. In 1581, he constructed a castle, centered on a three-story donjon on the grounds occupied by the daimyo whom he had defeated, which became the basis for the present Himeji Castle.

Definite information on the donjon of this castle had been lacking, but during recent repairs on the castle, excavation of the stone foundation on which the present donjon stands brought to light another stone foundation dating from Hideyoshi's time. The older foundation was slightly smaller and lower, measuring 15.75 meters by 15.75 meters at the upper bed of the stone wall, and had a cellar 2 meters

deep at the center. At the Ri gate (Fig. 34), one of the ceiling boards was found to bear the inscription "five carpenters, 1599." At that time, the castle was occupied by Kinoshita Iesada (1543–1608), elder brother of Hideyoshi's wife, who had been given the castle in 1585. The renovation in 1599 was not directly supervised by Hideyoshi, who had died the preceding year, but his ideas were carried out by Iesada. In addition, other stone foundations, including that surrounding the inner moat called Sangoku (Figs 18, 35), bear the marks of earlier construction methods; and numerous other traces of the castle as it existed during Hideyoshi's time have been discovered.

The present Himeji Castle was built by the son-in-law of Tokugawa Ieyasu, Ikeda Terumasa (1564–1613), as a defense against the daimyos hostile to the Tokugawa government. As a reward for his exploits in the Battle of Sekigahara, he was

33. *Aerial view of top story of main donjon of Himeji Castle. Completed 1609. Himeji, Hyogo Prefecture. (See also Figure 30.)*

entrusted with governing the western provinces. As soon as he took over the castle, Terumasa set about renovating it completely. The work, begun in 1601, took almost nine years to complete. By removing Hideyoshi's three-story donjon, expanding the foundation to 25.6 meters (from east to west) by 19.7 meters (from north to south), and building a new five-story, seven-floor donjon surrounded by three additional small donjons, the castle was made exceedingly formidable (Figs. 32, 45).

These donjons were all connected by fortified two-story corridors (Fig. 30), and kitchen facilities were built in the donjon complex in preparation for siege (Fig. 27). Two- or three-story turrets, placed at all the strategic points, were connected with one another by fortified corridors (Fig. 46). The walls of the castle itself were made of wooden frames several feet thick, which were filled in with

bamboo lath and clay; and the eaves were covered with plaster and whitewashed as protection against rain and fire. All the windows were made of vertical slats (Fig. 33), and those on the top floor were made largest to permit a good view of the surrounding countryside.

Himeji Castle is representative of castle construction at its peak, in regard to both its defense structures and its general design. The donjon of Himeji Castle was one of the most heavily fortified donjons built. In order to enter the donjon complex several gates had to be passed, and even if invaders successfully broke through all these gates, they would only gain entry to a yard where they would encounter an assault from four donjons and the connecting corridors.

One can get some idea of the original appearance of Hideyoshi's Osaka Castle from the plans (Fig.

34. *Ri Gate and turret of Himeji Castle. 1599. Himeji, Hyogo Prefecture.*

35. *Sangoku Moat of Himeji Castle. Himeji, Hyogo Prefecture.*

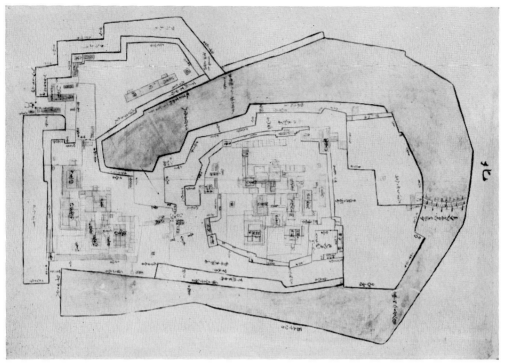

*36. Ground plan of Hideyoshi's Osaka Castle (north is to right). Collection of Tadashige Nakai.*

36) handed down in the Nakai family, and from the screens (Fig. 39) depicting the Sieges of Osaka Castle, originally executed for the Kuroda family and currently owned by the castle museum. There are also descriptions of the donjon in the records dated March 16, 1586, left by Gaspar Coelho (c.1530–90), a Jesuit priest who had been received in audience by Hideyoshi.

The donjon is also mentioned in the records of the daimyo Otomo Sorin (1530–87), who went to Osaka to consult with Hideyoshi about the invasion of his domain, Bungo Province (present-day Oita Prefecture), by the daimyo Shimazu Yoshihisa (1533–1614) of Satsuma Province (part of present-day Kagoshima Prefecture). According to these records, the donjon was filled with gold, silver, silk, brocades, and expensive tea utensils. In one room there were stocks of swords and daggers;

and in another room was a large, long chest that contained the parts of a portable golden tearoom, the ruler's special pride. The top floor seemed to be for observation purposes and had none of these treasures in it; and as for its size, Coelho records that when his group of thirty missionaries was seated, some of the men's clothing touched Hideyoshi. Coelho also reported that the top railings of the balusters surrounding that floor had raised tips.

Frois, in a description written in 1584, notes that Hideyoshi's Osaka Castle had five towers, the main one being a nine-story structure; that the castle could be seen from afar; and that it was conspicuously opulent and pompous. The donjon seems to have been used mainly as a storehouse: there is no record of its having reception rooms and interior decorations. Reception rooms were, however, built in the palace not far from the donjon; and the

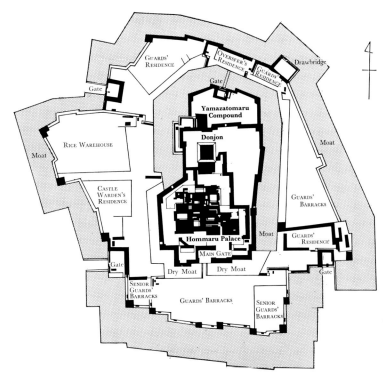

Labels on plan: GUARDS' RESIDENCE · OVERSEER'S RESIDENCE · GUARDS' RESIDENCE · Drawbridge · Gate · Gate · Yamazatomaru Compound · Donjon · Moat · RICE WAREHOUSE · Moat · CASTLE WARDEN'S RESIDENCE · GUARDS' BARRACKS · GUARDS' RESIDENCE · Moat · Hommaru Palace · MAIN GATE · Gate · Dry Moat · Dry Moat · Gate · SENIOR GUARDS' BARRACKS · GUARDS' BARRACKS · SENIOR GUARDS' BARRACKS

*37. Ground plan of Osaka Castle around 1630, according to specifications in documents owned by Tadashige Nakai. (See also Figure 124.)*

interiors of these rooms were decorated with beautiful murals depicting various birds, landscapes, legendary episodes of Japanese and Chinese history, and other subjects. In describing their meetings with Hideyoshi, Frois and Otomo mention that three reception rooms, each eighteen tatami mats in size, had been made into one large audience suite by the temporary removal of the *fusuma*. Colorful birds, flowers, and trees on a gold-colored ground had been painted on the *fusuma* of this room, and it was in the elevated section of this gorgeous audience suite that Hideyoshi sat. In his Osaka Castle, Hideyoshi combined residential quarters emphasizing interior decoration with a donjon stressing exterior design.

Among the other famous castles and their donjons built, like Hideyoshi's Osaka Castle, before the Battle of Sekigahara and no longer in existence

are: Okayama Castle (Fig. 8); Aizu-Wakamatsu Castle (1592), Fukushima Prefecture; Azuchi Castle (Fig. 28), Shiga Prefecture; Hideyoshi's Fushimi Castle; and the castle that Shibata Katsuie, who served Nobunaga as a general with Hideyoshi, built in Kitanosho, in present-day Fukui Prefecture. The donjons known to us or existing from the pre-Sekigahara years are indeed few, and the list is not impressive even if one includes those that were not destroyed until World War II: Maruoka Castle (Fig. 53), Fukui Prefecture; Okayama Castle; Hiroshima Castle; and Matsumoto Castle (Figs. 42, 43), Nagano Prefecture.

In contrast, many donjons built after the Battle of Sekigahara still survive—for example, the seventeenth-century donjons of Inuyama Castle (Fig. 11), Aichi Prefecture; Hikone Castle (Fig. 41), Shiga Prefecture; Himeji Castle (Fig. 32), Hyogo

38. *Aerial view of present Osaka Castle.*

Prefecture; Matsue Castle (Fig. 58), Shimane Prefecture; Uwajima Castle (Fig. 62), Ehime Prefecture; and Marugame Castle (Fig. 44), Kagawa Prefecture. In addition, Bitchu-Matsuyama Castle (Fig. 13), Okayama Prefecture; Kochi Castle (Fig. 63), Kochi Prefecture; Hirosaki Castle (Fig. 15), Aomori Prefecture; and Iyo-Matsuyama Castle (Fig. 12), Ehime Prefecture, all still have their donjons. However, the seventeenth-century donjons of Kubota Castle, Akita Prefecture; Kokura Castle, Fukuoka Prefecture; Tsuyama Castle (Fig. 23), Okayama Prefecture; and Bingo-Fukuyama Castle, Hiroshima Prefecture, together with that of Hagi Castle (Fig. 50), Yamaguchi Prefecture, survived only until the Meiji Restoration in 1868.

Since the *yamajiro* had few structures to begin with, the remains of stone foundations and walls are usually all that exist. But the *hirayamajiro* and the *hirajiro* had numerous structures—such as turrets, gates, fences, and moats—and many of them still maintain their original beautiful appearance. There are many castle grounds, among them Edo Castle, that despite the loss of the donjon retain enough of their original structures to suggest the appearance of the castle complex and that of the donjon.

Tokugawa Ieyasu chose the small town of Edo—which developed into the city of Tokyo—as his military base and built Edo Castle, the largest in Japan, after he was appointed daimyo of the Kanto area (the area surrounding Edo) in 1590 by Toyotomi Hideyoshi. This great castle, completed in 1606, became the headquarters of the Tokugawa shoguns and the center of autocratic centralized government for more than two hundred and fifty years. The castle had concentric circles of wide moats and massive walls and gates, and the outermost circle had a diameter of over three kilometers.

39. *Osaka Castle and main donjon in screen depicting siege of Osaka Castle in the summer of 1614. Seventeenth century. Osaka Castle Museum.*

40. Screen depicting *Juraku-dai castle-palace*. Late six-teenth century. Collection of Mitsui family, Tokyo. *(See also Figures 4, 69.)*

41. *Donjon of Hikone Castle. Moved to present site 1606. Hikone, Shiga Prefecture. (See also Figure 54.)*

42. *Matsumoto Castle: in front of main donjon are attached turrets and to right is small donjon connected to main donjon by covered corridor. 1597. Matsumoto, Nagano Prefecture. (See also Figures 26, 43.)*

43 (overleaf, left). Main donjon of Matsumoto Castle, with attached turrets in right foreground. ▷
1597. Matsumoto, Nagano Prefecture. (See also Figures 26, 42.)

45. *Himeji Castle. Completed 1609. Himeji, Hyogo Prefecture.*

◁ *46. Fortified corridor and Ni Gate of Himeji Castle. Completed 1609. Himeji, Hyogo Prefecture.*

*47. The Fujimi (Fuji-Viewing) Turret of Edo Castle. Nineteenth century. Tokyo.*

The donjon and the buildings located in the *hommaru* (main) compound were for the shogun's use; the *ninomaru* and *sannomaru* (second and third) compounds contained rooms in which his family and other household members resided, receptions were held, and administrative matters were attended to. Nearby, but separated by a moat and walls, was the Western Castle (now the Imperial Palace of Tokyo), where the shogun's son or the retired shogun lived; and behind this castle was a park for the castle residents. Most of the buildings, including the donjon, no longer exist, and of the towers and gates that remain, only one or two date back to the early Edo period. Nevertheless, in Tokyo today, the pine trees growing on the well-tended grounds and the reflections of the stone walls and white towers in the moats (Figs. 17, 47, 48) evoke images of the castle that once reigned supreme.

Kumamoto Castle (Figs. 14, 51) also retains many of its turrets, gates, and fences, although the main and side towers were lost during the Satsuma Rebellion of 1877, led by Saigo Takamori (1827–77), against the Meiji government. The high stone foundation, which slopes gracefully down from the turrets and parapets, is particularly beautiful.

Other castles that retain some of the original structures include the Kanazawa (Figs. 16, 52; Ishikawa Prefecture), Osaka, Nagoya, Nijo, Takamatsu (Kagawa Prefecture), Ozu (Ehime Prefecture), Fukuyama (Hiroshima Prefecture), Okayama, Akashi (Hyogo Prefecture), and Ueda (Nagano Prefecture) castles. Unique among them is Kanazawa Castle, whose turrets have tiles on the lower parts of the outer walls (Fig. 52).

**TOKUGAWA POLICY** The Tokugawa government, established in 1603 by Tokugawa Ieyasu, promulgated various laws during the Genna and Kan'ei eras (1615–44) in attempts to consolidate its power by further increasing its control over the warriors and the

*48. Earthen- and stone-walled inner moat of Edo Castle. Seventeenth century. Tokyo. (See also Figures 17, 47.)*

daimyos. In 1615 the government ordered the daimyos to destroy all but one of the castles within their domains. Consequently, border forts and branch castles were destroyed, leaving only the castle in which the daimyo resided. The Tokugawa government also prohibited the rebuilding and even the repair of a castle unless permission was obtained beforehand. As decades passed, some of the castles and donjons that had not been destroyed by fire or other disasters became badly run down from lack of funds for repair. Since poor maintenance of the castle was tantamount to announcing a daimyo's financial difficulties to the residents of his domain, it could lead to loss of the daimyo's authority. Consequently, the Tokugawa government, which had severely restricted castle construction and repair work, had to provide the daimyos with large financial subsidies for necessary repair work so that they would not lose face.

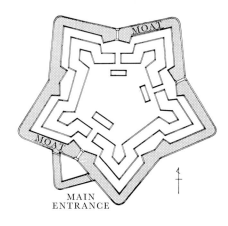

*49. Ground plan of Goryokaku, built in Hakodate, Hokkaido, in 1860.*

*50. Donjon of Hagi Castle in Yamaguchi Prefecture. Completed 1608; dismantled 1873.*

Most of the castles rebuilt during the Edo period were either smaller than or exact copies of earlier structures, with few innovative features. Toward the end of the Edo period, Western techniques of finishing and laying stone and the more regular floor plans of the West were incorporated in Japanese castle building, resulting in a few castles with interesting designs: for example, Goryokaku (Fig. 49), a pentacle-shaped fortress at Hakodate in Hokkaido; Tatsuoka Castle, in Nagano Prefecture; and the Odaiba, a military base that the Tokugawa government built in Tokyo Bay to strengthen the defense of Edo.

The Edo (Fig. 6), Osaka (Fig. 5), and Nijo (Fig. 7) castles, built as official residences of the Tokugawas, had complexes of opulent structures in which audiences were held and imperial messengers and foreign ambassadors received. By the Meiji Restoration in 1868, all three of these castles had lost their donjons and only the massive stone foundations were left to remind the viewer of the past. The donjon of Edo Castle, the Tokugawa headquarters, burned during the great Meireki fire of January 18–19, 1657, and was never rebuilt. The donjon of Osaka Castle was struck by lightning and burned on January 2, 1665, less than forty years after it was constructed. The donjon of Nijo Castle, which had been built as a gesture for the imperial visit in 1626, burned in August, 1750, after being struck by lightning. Konchi-in Suden (1569–1633), a scholarly monk and government official, described this donjon in the *Record of the Imperial Visit in Kan'ei,* an account he coauthored with Karasumaru Mitsuhiro in 1626: "The fabulous donjon soars thirty meters—it seemed as if we could almost touch the stars, and we were afraid that our voices would startle the people of heaven."

*Chitose no Matsu* (Pine Trees of Chitose), a biog-

51. *Main turret of Kumamoto Castle. 1607. Kumamoto City, Kumamoto Prefecture. (See also Figure 14.)*

raphy of Hoshina Masayuki (1611–72), a close relative of one of the Tokugawa shoguns, written in 1828, gives the reasons that the donjon of Edo Castle was not rebuilt during the general restoration of the castle after the Meireki fire. By the autumn of 1659 the construction work on all the structures of Edo Castle had been completed. The donjon, however, was not rebuilt because Hoshina Masayuki presented a convincing argument when its reconstruction came up for discussion. He felt that reconstruction of the donjon should be postponed indefinitely, since it had existed merely as a decorative structure and did not contribute much to the fortification of the castle. He further argued that prolonging the construction work would have adverse economic effects. Vast expenditures for a donjon could no longer be easily sustained by the government.

A similar account appears in the section on

Hoshina Masayuki in *Kansei Jushu Shokafu,* an 1812 compilation of genealogies and family histories of prominent daimyos and governmental officials. Behind Masayuki's recommendation lay the general understanding that the Tokugawa government had already firmly established itself and that in such peaceful times there was no need to build a donjon merely to display the government's authority.

In the early years of their rule, the Tokugawas had provided the daimyos in charge of government-related construction with both money and supplies of wood: the daimyos were responsible only for recruiting laborers. But for the reconstruction of Edo Castle after the Meireki fire, the daimyos had the additional burdens of paying the carpenters recruited for the work and providing food for them. Under Tokugawa rule, the economic burden for the construction of imperial structures, as well as the construction and rebuilding of the

52. *Fortification of Ishikawa Gate of Kanazawa Castle. 1788. Kanazawa, Ishikawa Prefecture. (See also Figure 16.)*

53. *Donjon of Maruoka Castle. 1576. Maruoka, Fukui Prefecture. (See also Figures 19, 20.)*

Edo Castle structures, had been assigned to most of the daimyos; but as such work assignments continued to be made, only such wealthy daimyos as Ikeda of Bizen Province (present-day Okayama Prefecture), Asano of Aki Province (present-day Hiroshima Prefecture), Datè of Rikuzen Province (present-day Miyagi Prefecture), and Shimazu of Satsuma Province (present-day Kagoshima Prefecture) could take on the costly jobs.

Bankruptcy was predictable for most daimyos, because they were forced to pay for the construction and rebuilding of not only the Edo, Osaka, and Nijo castles, and the frequently rebuilt imperial palaces, but also the castles of the sons of shoguns. The original purpose behind this government policy had been to weaken the economic power of the uncommitted daimyos; but by the latter half of the seventeenth century the effects had gone too far, and many daimyos were facing financial crises. Under these circumstances, money could not be wasted on a donjon intended only for display.

SURVIVING DONJONS Only twelve donjons remain unchanged from feudal times; and beginning in northern Japan and moving south, they are found in the following castles: Hirosaki, Matsumoto, Maruoka, Hikone, Inuyama, Himeji (which we have already discussed), Matsue, Bitchu-Matsuyama, Marugame, Iyo-Matsuyama, Uwajima, and Kochi. As was mentioned earlier, almost all these extant donjons were built after the Battle of Sekigahara.

Hirosaki Castle was originally a frontier fort in the Tsugaru plain (western Aomori Prefecture), and was used by the Tsugarus, a daimyo family, as their base from 1610 until the end of the Edo period. The donjon, completed in 1611, was struck

54. *Fortified entrance to Hommaru Compound of Hikone Castle; bridge spans steep moatlike ravine and road to castle. Hikone, Shiga Prefecture. (See also Figure 41.)*

by lightning and burned. It was left in ruins until the present three-story donjon (Fig. 15) was built on the southeast corner of the main compound in 1810. Although the exterior of the donjon has single-dormer-gabled roofs, the interior of the building lacks any decorative consideration. The two unique features of this castle are the horse-chestnut shingles used on the roofs as protection against the extreme cold and the castle moat, whose sides are made of earth rather than of stone.

The donjon of Matsumoto Castle (Figs. 26, 42) was built in 1597. The castle, located in the middle of the Matsumoto plain (a commercial and political center in Nagano Prefecture since the Muromachi period), was built by one of the warriors who served the Ogasawara family of daimyos; and the present five-story, six-floor donjon was erected by the daimyo Ishikawa Yasunaga. For its defense, this typical *hirajiro* takes full advantage of the river running close by. A group of three towers is situated at the southwest corner of the main compound; because

of the heavy snows the towers have few ornamental gables and the hipped roofs all have different pitches. This revolutionary technique to ease the burden of the snows was far in advance of architectural techniques of the times. The walls, covered with black wooden panels as insulation, contain numerous apertures for shooting from and for hurling stones (Fig. 43).

The donjon of Maruoka Castle (Figs. 20, 53) in Fukui Prefecture was built in 1576. After quelling the Ikko uprising in 1576 (an uprising of the followers of the Ikko sect of Buddhism in the Hokuriku district), Oda Nobunaga sent Shibata Katsuie's adopted son to govern this area and had him build the castle that became the original structure of the Maruoka Castle complex. The donjon, the oldest surviving one, has a watchtower on its roof (Fig. 19). After the Meiji Restoration, maintenance of the castle was neglected and consequently the castle deteriorated; in 1948 it collapsed during an earthquake. The present structure was rebuilt from

55. Donjon of Inuyama Castle, overlooking Kiso River. 1600. Inuyama, Aichi Prefecture. (See also Figures 11, 56.)

56 (below, left). Tokonoma and chigaidana in master's reception suite in donjon of Inuyama Castle. 1600; reconstructed, nineteenth century. Inuyama. Aichi Prefecture. (See also Figures 11, 55.)

57 (below, right). Interior of main donjon of Himeji Castle; the double row of pegs on the wall was used as a gun rack. Completed 1609. Himeji, Hyogo Prefecture. (See also Figures 30, 33.)

*58. Donjon of Matsue Castle. 1611. Matsue, Shimane Prefecture. (See also Figure 25.)*

the original materials. The roof tiles of the donjon are made of stone, one measure devised as protection against extreme cold.

The donjon of Hikone Castle (Fig. 41) was moved to Shiga Prefecture in 1606. The castle, the residence of Ii Naosuke (1815–60), a chief Tokugawa administrator who was assassinated just outside Edo Castle in 1860, was constructed by one of Naosuke's ancestors, Ii Naokatsu. The donjon is believed to have been built in 1575 and moved from a castle near Otsu. Although the donjon has only three floors and is relatively small, the harmoniously intersecting gables give it a complex design. The four corners on the first story are decorated with dormer gables and the top story has a *karahafu*-gabled roof. The many windows of various sizes admit a great deal of light, making the interior bright; and as a decorative element, those on the two upper floors are arched. Hikone Castle retains many turrets (Fig. 54) and is one of the few complete castle complexes remaining today.

The donjon of Inuyama Castle (Figs. 11, 55), built in 1600 in Aichi Prefecture, was originally a two-story building with a two-story watchtower added above. It was long believed that this four-story, five-floor donjon had been built in 1537 and brought from Kanayama Castle in Gifu Prefecture to Inuyama Castle in 1599. But recent repair work revealed no trace of such a move. Moreover, the reception suite (Fig. 56) in the donjon is now considered to have been made during the Edo period. The donjon, standing on a small hill by the Kiso River on the outskirts of Inuyama City, once presented a picturesque site, but its scenic beauty has been seriously impaired by the recent construction of a hotel and a dam.

The donjon of Matsue Castle (Fig. 58) was built in 1611 in Shimane Prefecture by Horio Yoshiharu (1543–1611), who was given Izumo and Oki provinces (both in present-day Shimane Prefecture) as reward for his exploits in the Battle of Sekigahara. During the administrative changes of the Meiji era (1868–1912), most of the structures on the castle grounds were destroyed and only the donjon remains. The donjon has five stories and six floors and is relatively large, but its construction is much simpler than that of Himeji Castle, built about the same time. The donjon of Matsue Castle, con-

59. *Donjon of Marugame Castle. Seventeenth century. Marugame, Kagawa Prefecture. (See also Figure 44.)*

60. *Stone foundations and sixth turret of Osaka Castle. Seventeenth century. Osaka.*

61. *Iyo-Matsuyama Castle. 1854. Matsuyama, Ehime Prefecture. (See also Figure 12.)*

structed in a much older style, is actually a three-story watchtower built on a two-story structure with a double roof. The only turret is, in fact, the entrance to the donjon (Fig. 25).

The donjon of Bitchu-Matsuyama Castle (Fig. 13) was constructed in 1683 in Takahashi, Okayama Prefecture, by the daimyo Mizutani Katsumune (d. 1693). From medieval times this area was considered strategically important because it connected central Japan to the western regions. The castle, originally built atop a nearby hill (Fig. 1), was moved to its present location toward the end of the sixteenth century and was extensively renovated in 1600 by the celebrated Kobori Enshu (1579–1647), who was then known as Masakazu and was one of the administrators of the Tokugawa estates. This small two-story structure resembles a *yamajiro* in that it stands on a low stone foundation raised on natural rock. The top floor of the donjon has space set aside for a Buddhist altar.

The donjon of Marugame Castle (Fig. 44) was built in the seventeenth century in present-day Kagawa Prefecture in Shikoku. This castle was demolished in compliance with the Tokugawa policy of allowing only one castle per feudal domain, but in 1641 it was rebuilt by Yamazaki Ieharu, the daimyo of Kai Province (present-day Yamanashi Prefecture). Then, beginning in 1642 and continuing for more than thirty years, Ieharu gradually expanded the castle grounds to their present size. Unfortunately a fire in 1869 burned all the buildings except the donjon and the first and second gates. The three-story donjon has *karahafu* and dormer gables decorating the roof of the first story, and a boxlike structure used for dropping stones protrudes at one corner. The layers of stone foundations built on the castle hill are especially attractive, and from the town below, the donjon looks unexpectedly imposing for its small size.

Toyotomi Hideyoshi installed the daimyo Kato

62. Donjon, with formal entrance, of Uwajima Castle. 1665. Uwajima, Ehime Prefecture.

63. Donjon of Kochi Castle. 1747. Kochi City, Kochi Prefecture.

Yoshiaki (1563–1631) in Iyo Province (present-day Ehime Prefecture) for assisting in his invasions of Korea in the late sixteenth century. Iyo-Matsuyama Castle, which Yoshiaki began to construct in 1601, had a donjon with five stories. This donjon was rebuilt in 1624 but was struck by lightning in 1784. The present donjon (Fig. 12) was built in 1854. The black wooden walls and the almost straight dormer gables and roofs (Fig. 61) are quite striking; and the overall structure and design of this valuable building are characteristic of the architecture of the Edo period. The castle had the same tower formation as Himeji Castle, but the three small donjons were burned by an arsonist in 1933, and only the main donjon remains today.

In 1665 in present-day Ehime Prefecture, Shikoku, a grandson of the powerful daimyo Datè Masamune (1566–1636) of Sendai in northern Honshu, built the donjon of Uwajima Castle (Fig. 62). Unlike the other donjons we have discussed,

the Uwajima Castle donjon is smaller than its stone foundation, and a part of the upper bed of the foundation is visible all the way around the donjon structure. Moreover, this donjon has a formal entrance gate with a *karahafu*-gabled roof. Because it is devoid of any defensive structures, such as trapdoors for dropping stones and apertures used for firing on an attacker, we can surmise that the donjon must have been built during rather peaceful times.

The original donjon of Kochi Castle in present-day Kochi Prefecture, Shikoku, burned in 1729 and the present donjon (Fig. 63) was built in exact duplication of the original. The castle was constructed by the daimyo who was installed in Tosa Province (present-day Kochi Prefecture) for his part in the Battle of Sekigahara. The donjon, with a two-story watchtower built atop a two-story turret, is similar to the donjons of Inuyama and Maruoka castles.

# CHAPTER TWO

# The Warrior Residences

**THE SHOIN** Because of the many meanings it has acquired over the centuries, the term *shoin* can be quite confusing. In China, a *shoin* was a building the emperor provided for his scholars. During Japan's middle ages (that is, from the late twelfth century to the early seventeenth century) the term was frequently used to refer to a room in which to read. In a Buddhist temple it was a monk's private study or living room, and the built-in writing table in the shallow bay of the room (Fig. 64), which extended onto the veranda, was also called a *shoin*. It is this shallow bay that developed into the alcove we call the *tsukeshoin;* and the broad sill of the window in the *tsukeshoin* is, of course, the vestige of the built-in writing table.

In the middle ages the warrior class built *shoin* rooms in their residences to be used for studying Japanese classics and Chinese texts and for meditating. Since these rooms came to be used for receiving guests, reception rooms also acquired the name *shoin*. Sometimes the inner part of a *shoin* reception room was raised as a dais (*jodan*), to be used only by persons of the highest rank. On the wall behind the *jodan* were a wooden-floored tokonoma (which was decorated with pictures, flowers, and so on, and sometimes had a raised, tatami-matted floor) and the *chigaidana* (the adjoining ornamental shelves). It is not surprising, then, that *shoin* designates not only a reception room but also a building with a reception room in the *shoin* style.

The history of architecture was established as a field of learning in the Meiji era, and the *shoin* was then defined as a type of residential structure built from the end of the middle ages through the Edo period. In an encyclopedia published by Heibonsha in 1932, Dr. Yasushi Tanabe defines *shoin* as "a type of Japanese residential structure that developed during the end of the Muromachi period [1336–1568]. At first, *shoin* referred to either a study or a lecture hall in a temple, but since *shoin* were also used for receiving guests, the term came to signify this room, as well. As the aristocrats, warriors, and priests adopted similar styles of living, the *shoin* rooms that had first been built in Buddhist temple complexes during the Kamakura period [1185–1336] were also built by the aristocrats and warriors in their residences. A building constructed in the *shoin* style is characterized by having a *genkan* [front entrance] and a room that is equipped with such decorative elements as a tokonoma, *chigaidana*, and a *tsukeshoin*. The style continued to develop throughout the Edo period and was finally incorporated into the contemporary Japanese residence." Until recent research established that the Edo period was well advanced before the use of the *genkan* became prevalent in residences, Dr. Tanabe's definition of the *shoin* was generally accepted. If the *genkan* is to be made part of the *shoin* style, however, the beginnings of this style must date only from the Edo period.

The three room decorations—the tokonoma, *chigaidana*, and the *tsukeshoin*—are usually men-

64. *An early* shoin *extending onto the veranda, as depicted in the fourteenth-century picture scroll* Honen Shonin Eden *(A Pictorial Biography of Saint Honen).*

tioned in various theories as being basic to the *shoin* room; and there are usually other elements, such as square pillars, floors covered with tatami, *fusuma* (sliding partitions made of opaque paper on both sides of a wooden frame and used as room dividers), and *shoji* (sliding panels made of translucent paper on one side of a latticed wooden frame and used as windows or doors). Another definition, given in *Dai Genkai*, a 1932 dictionary of the Japanese language, describes the *shoin* as a type of room structure that uses both *fusuma* and *shoji*.

In *Nihon Kenchikushi Josetsu* (An Introduction to the History of Japanese Architecture), Dr. Hirotaro Ota synthesizes recent studies and writes: "As can be seen in the diagrams of the residences depicted in the volume on palaces and residences in the *Shomei* [a five-volume handbook on carpentry

and design techniques prepared in 1608 by the Heinouchi family, who served the Tokugawas as the head carpentry supervisors in the Edo area], the *shoin* does have a definite floor plan. This style, adopted by the daimyos in their residences during the Edo period, places the quarters for servants near the center of the residence [see foldout facing page 72]. Adjoining this section are both the quarters for guests and the residential section. The distinctive feature is that approximately one-third of the entire area is devoted to quarters for guests. The most important part of the residence was the *ohiroma* [formal reception hall] with an innermost section that had a *jodan*, a tokonoma, *chigaidana*, a *tsukeshoin*, and *chodaigamae* [decorated doors]. There was a *chumon* [short, open inner corridor; Fig. 77] serving as the entrance to the reception hall; this

*65. Illustration from* Nenju Gyoji Emaki *(Picture Scroll of Annual Events) showing the typical southern frontage of a* shinden *structure. Twelfth century.*

*chumon* was connected to the corridor-like veranda of the hall. The *chumon* was replaced when a separate entrance building developed."

**TATAMI AND SEATING LEVELS** Status differences in the Edo period were indicated quite clearly through the use of rooms in the audience suite with different floor levels: the *jodan* (with the highest elevation), the *chudan* (with a lower elevation), and the *gedan* (with the lowest elevation). Indicating status through seating arrangements on differing levels was a very old practice. During the Heian period (794–1185) the main building consisted of three sections: the core (the central, inner area), the broad corridor-like veranda, and the area under the eaves. The seating arrangement used during formal receptions and on other ceremonial occasions was always determined according to social rank: the

places farthest from the core indicated lower status.

The formal seat for the master in an aristocrat's mansion was located in the core; he sat on two tatami laid side by side on the wooden floor with another smaller and thinner tatami laid atop them. This arrangement is still seen in the Seiryo-den (Fig. 66) of the Imperial Palace in Kyoto. The floor of the corridor-like veranda was one level lower than that of the core; and the area under the eaves, two levels lower than the core-area floor, was practically exposed to the weather. Chairs, mats, and round cushions were placed in the central area and in the area under the eaves, because the entire floor was made of wood. It was not until much later that the wooden floor was entirely covered with tatami.

On important ceremonial occasions—as, for instance, the banquet held when the master of the house received an appointment as minister—tatami

66. *Eastern section of Seiryo-den, looking toward the courtyard; the dais of two tatami mats is for the emperor's use. 1855. Kyoto Imperial Palace. (See also Figure 67.)*

mats were placed in the core. Along with the master, guests of high rank were seated here, while those of lower rank were seated elsewhere on thin round cushions made of woven straw rope. The thickness and shape of the cushions and mats, as well as the kinds of materials used to make them, indicated differences in status. Scenes depicting arrangements like these are found in numerous picture scrolls dating from early times, such as the *Nenju Gyoji Emaki* (Picture Scroll of Annual Events; Fig. 65), painted during the late Heian period, and the *Kasuga Gongen Reigenki* (The Origin and Miracles of the Kasuga Shrine), painted in the early 1300s.

An early description of the use of tatami for important occasions appears in "The Account of the Shogun's Visit to the Residence of the Honorable Miyoshi Yoshinaga, Titular Governor of Chikuzen" in *Gunsho Ruiju*, an exhaustive collection of classical writings compiled by Hanawa Hokinoichi

(1746–1821). This document records the visit of Yoshiteru (1535–65), the thirteenth Ashikaga shogun, to Yoshinaga's residence on March 30, 1561. There are floor plans (Fig. 70) and illustrations depicting the various receptions held in the main hall. This account uses two area-measurement units: *ma*, to refer to the principal rooms, and *jo*, to refer to the less significant rooms. The term *ma*, which refers to the space between two pillars, had been used to designate the size of an area prior to the time when floors were covered with tatami; *jo* is used when indicating the actual number of tatami mats in a room.

The rooms chosen to receive the shogun in were two reception rooms in the main hall—the inner four-*ma* room and the nine-*ma* room that faced west. In referring to the four-*ma* room used as the shogunal seat during the visit, the account mentions that "the armor and other items were placed

67. *Court officials' office on south side of Seiryo-den; thin tatami mats are placed around work tables as seats. 1855. Kyoto Imperial Palace. (See also Figure 66.)*

directly on the mats" and that "every one of the mats had silk borders decorated with a Korean design"—suggesting that for important occasions a room whose entire floor was covered with mats was used. The four-*ma* room, which measured two *ma* by two *ma*, was the room in which Yoshinaga and his aides had the honor of participating in ceremonial drinking with the visiting shogun. It had a tokonoma of plain boards one and a half *ma* wide, *chigaidana* one-half *ma* wide, and *chodaigamae* two *ma* wide. In front of the *chodaigamae* an additional mat with silk borders was laid as the shogunal seat.

After the ceremonial drinking Yoshinaga presented the shogun with two swords; this was followed by the shogun's customary inspection of some horses. The shogun then entered the nine-*ma* room. On the east side of this room was a plain-board tokonoma two *ma* wide, decorated with

three pictures, a flower vase, and other articles. The shogun was seated on a mat placed in front of the tokonoma. Before him, to his right and left, were his aides and Yoshinaga. Ceremonial drinking again took place while a Noh drama was performed on the stage in the garden. The Noh performance was viewed by the shogun's accompanying retainers, who were seated in the adjoining room, in the four-*jo* room east of the stable, and in the garden.

As we have already seen, the use of tatami, thin mats, and coarse mats was an important means of indicating status differences. *A Secret Record of Historical Facts on the Buddhist School,* prepared early in the Edo period and handed down at Nishi Hongan-ji temple in Kyoto, says about the school that "the audience suite did not have a *jodan.* Only tatami had been placed in the space within the floor frame where the retinue was to be seated. Near the frame

# Daimyo Residences in Edo

The Asano family, daimyos of Aki Province (present-day Hiroshima Prefecture), maintained its official residence just outside the Sakurada Gate of Edo Castle. In addition to private residences, the family owned residential land in other parts of Edo, including Aoyama and Tsukiji. This ground plan from the Hiroshima Municipal Asano Library shows the official residence rebuilt after the fire of 1731. The ochre-colored sections were for the use of the daimyo, and the brown-colored sections were for the use of his wife.

Because Asano Yoshinaga (d. 1752) married the daughter of a shogun, a *goshuden* was built for his wife. The *goshuden* was an extensive residence for a shogun's daughter who was to marry a daimyo of the Third or higher rank. Customarily, the front gate of a *goshuden* was painted vermilion. The Lady's Quarters of the residence shown in the ground plan here are so grand as to rival the daimyo's own quarters; however, the Lady's Quarters of an ordinary daimyo residence were not usually built on such a lavish scale.

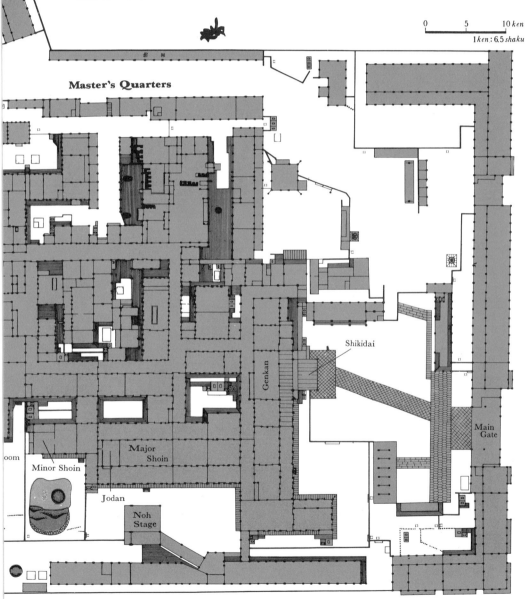

0    5    10 *ken*

1 *ken* : 6.5 *shaku*

**Master's Quarters**

Shikidai

Genkan

Main Gate

oom

Minor Shoin

Major Shoin

Jodan

Noh Stage

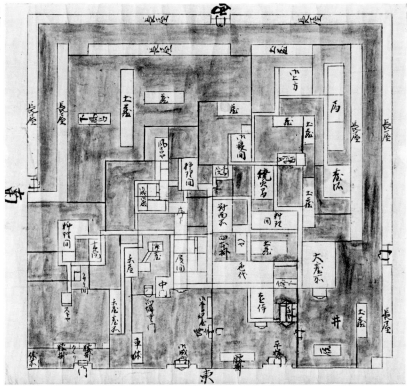

68. The Shomei *volume on palaces and residences and one of the ground plans of a typical daimyo residence appended to it. Seventeenth century. Tokyo University.*

were thin mats, farther out were coarse mats, and the outermost section was covered with split bamboo that had been nailed down. Until the priest Yuinyo rebuilt the audience suite in 1608, there was no *jodan,* but the place where the chief priest sat was set off by a single tatami. The tokonoma and other sections had paintings done in plain colors, none on a gold ground.''

The *Secret Record* notes that the practice of using additional tatami in the altar hall and in the audience suite to indicate high status began in 1536, when the temple was still in Osaka. In that year Nijo Haruyoshi and Ichijo Kanefuyu, two high-ranking court officials, went to Osaka to advise the abbot of Hongan-ji temple that he should be seated on additional tatami now that he had been appointed to a higher position. Until 1611, at the three-hundred-fiftieth anniversary of the founding of the sect by Honen, the thickness of the tatami

laid in the altar hall had been equal to that of two tatami. At the anniversary ceremony, the tatami was made thicker by ten to twelve centimeters, and eventually it became more than thirty centimeters thick.

The placement of tatami on the floor to create a dais for persons of high status eventually developed into the elevated section that we know as the *jodan.* The audience suites in the *ohiroma,* or formal reception hall, of Juraku-dai castle-palace and Sendai Castle, in the *hondo* (abbot's audience quarters; Fig. 152) of Zuigan-ji temple in Miyagi Prefecture, and in the *shiroshoin,* or formal *shoin,* of Kyoto's Nishi Hongan-ji temple (Figs. 96, 156) have an L-shaped *jodan* within the main room; and the rooms comprising the suites are usually divided by *fusuma.* The L-shaped elevated section was adjusted according to the size of the room and the number of persons expected. It is not known how close to the

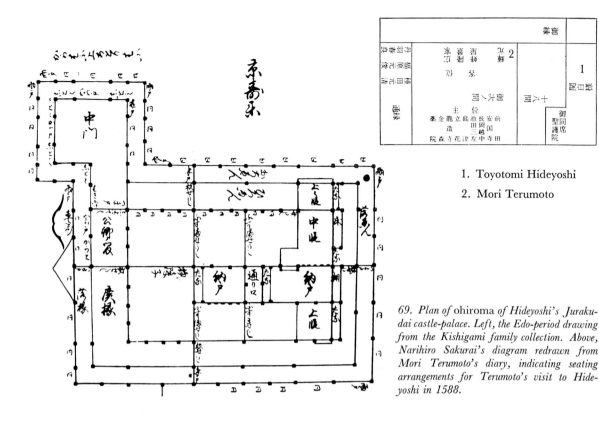

1. Toyotomi Hideyoshi

2. Mori Terumoto

*69. Plan of* ohiroma *of Hideyoshi's Juraku-dai castle-palace. Left, the Edo-period drawing from the Kishigami family collection. Above, Narihiro Sakurai's diagram redrawn from Mori Terumoto's diary, indicating seating arrangements for Terumoto's visit to Hideyoshi in 1588.*

master the subjects were allowed to sit, but we can assume that there was still a degree of leniency in regard to status and rank that allowed subjects to be near the person on the elevated section.

In 1585 Toyotomi Hideyoshi was made chief adviser to the emperor, in recognition of the fact that he was the most powerful man in the land. After building the Juraku-dai castle-palace (Figs. 4, 40) for himself in Kyoto in 1587, he requested and obtained a visit from Emperor Goyozei. Hideyoshi employed startling designs in Juraku-dai in his attempt to display his power and authority to the aristocrats and daimyos. According to one missionary's description, the exterior walls were decorated with gold and silver leaf and many carvings, and the roof tiles were framed in gold. The pillars in the *ohiroma* were described as emitting a fragrance, which must mean that they were not lacquered. There were three rows of rooms; the

audience suite used for formal receptions was located in the south row. The *jodan*, at one end of the audience suite, gave the room an L shape; and in it there were a tokonoma, *chigaidana*, a *tsukeshoin*, and *chodaigamae*. The north row of rooms was used for more informal receptions. Unfortunately, little is known of the actual appearance of the mansion, since the only materials providing us with clues are a few paintings, including the screens of Juraku-dai (Fig. 40) that are now owned by the Mitsui family and the plan of the *ohiroma* (Fig. 69) found among the documents of the Kishigami family. The screens depict a building appropriate for the *chumon* shown in the plans of the *ohiroma*.

*Taiko Ki,* a chronicle of Hideyoshi's life, describes the imperial visit in such detail that one can almost see Hideyoshi's triumphant mien; unfortunately, the book does not contain a single reference to the ceremonies performed or to the

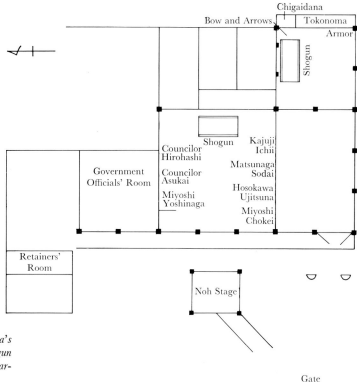

Chigaidana

Bow and Arrows

Tokonoma

Armor

Shogun

Shogun

Councilor
Hirohashi

Kajuji
Ichii

Government
Officials' Room

Councilor
Asukai

Matsunaga
Sodai

Miyoshi
Yoshinaga

Hosokawa
Ujitsuna

Miyoshi
Chokei

Retainers'
Room

Noh Stage

Gate

70. Plan of part of Miyoshi Yoshinaga's
residence at the time of the Ashikaga shogun
Yoshiteru's visit in 1561 indicating seating arrangements, according to Gunsho Ruiju.

entertainment provided for the emperor. In his
dissertation, the architectural historian Yoshikuni
Okuma presents Narihiro Sakurai's small diagram
of Hideyoshi's *ohiroma*, which indicates where the
participants sat on the occasion of the daimyo
Mori Terumoto's visit in 1588, well after he and
Hideyoshi had concluded peace. The diagram (Fig.
69) is from Terumoto's own diary and is valuable
in that it shows how an L-shaped *jodan* was actually
used. Hideyoshi sat in the center of the *jodan* and
the abbot of the Shogo-in temple sat in the projecting section. There are no documents that ex-
plain why this noble was seated there, but the
reason is not hard to conjecture. A diagram of the
seating arrangement used in Edo Castle in 1842 for
the visit of the messengers of the emperor, the
retired emperor, and the ministerial family, for
example, shows the Tokugawa heir, Iesada, sitting
in the same part of the room as did the abbot of

Shogo-in. The abbot, in other words, must have
been seated there because he accompanied Hideyoshi on that occasion.

In another description of how status differences
were indicated, *Gunsho Ruiju* records the visit of
Toyotomi Hideyoshi to the residence of the very
powerful daimyo Maeda Toshiie (1538–99) on
April 8, 1594, as follows: "While the leading Noh
actors of the Komparu, Kanze, Kongo, and Hosho
Noh schools staged various Noh plays, Toshiie
presented Hideyoshi with a bay horse and a sword
made by the distinguished swordsmith Nagamitsu.
In the meantime, a thirteen-course dinner was
served Hideyoshi by Deputy Etchu and the Chamberlain of the Left as the headwaiters and by
Deputy Asukai and Chamberlain Kanayama as
the wine stewards. Chamberlain Matsuto and
Chamberlain Noto were the storytellers. The abbot of the Shogo-in temple in Kyoto, the Minister

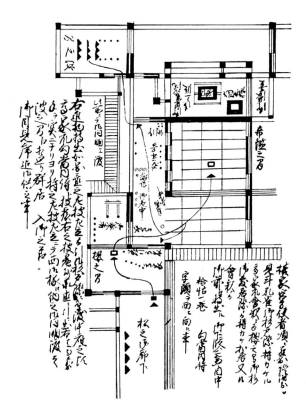

71. *A portion of Hotta's memorandum on protocol showing the shiroshoin in the Hommaru Compound of Edo Castle and containing detailed instructions for the New Year reception there. 1836.*

of the Right Kikutei, and the nobles accompanying Hideyoshi sat on the left and right of the *jodan.* On the right side of the *gedan* sat other nobles, including the Great Minister of Edo [Tokugawa Ieyasu], the Deputy Minister of Yamato Province, and Maeda Toshiie. On the left sat the court nobles, including the Great Minister of Kanju-ji in Kyoto, the Great Minister of Hirayama, and the Great Minister of Hino in Omi Province."

Eventually receptions came to be held in halls allowing for more space between the people involved, and relative status was expressed by seating people in large rooms with different floor levels. When it became necessary to set aside a larger area in residences for holding audiences, the simple placement of a dais in a room later developed into a two-room reception area containing a *jodan* and a *gedan.*

During the early Edo period, the *shoin*-style re-

ception halls of the Nijo, Osaka, and Edo castles were all decorated with a tokonoma, *chigaidana,* and a *tsukeshoin;* but differences in social status were expressed most clearly through the use of the *jodan.* The audience suite (Fig. 99) in the *ohiroma* in the Ninomaru Compound of the Nijo Castle complex can be regarded as one vast room of ninety-two mats, in the sense that the audience suite has neither doors nor *fusuma* between the forty-eight-mat *jodan* and the adjoining forty-four-mat *gedan.* Separation of the suite into two distinct rooms has been effected by the use of only two architectural devices: the black-lacquered sill between the different floor levels, and the small *kokabe,* or partial wall extending from the ceiling, between the two areas.

To effect further distinctions, an additional tatami could be placed on the floor of the *jodan,* as demonstrated in Figure 86. This was in fact done in Nijo Castle and in Edo Castle for the shogun

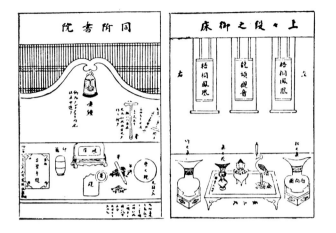

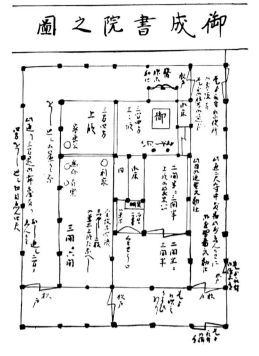

72. *Plan of* shoin *of Maeda Toshiie's residence from* Gunsho Ruiju, *purported to be a record of Toyotomi Hideyoshi's visit in 1594. Above, drawings indicating decorations and their placement in* tsukeshoin, *left, and tokonoma, right. Right, floor plan of* shoin *indicating seating arrangements. Cabinet Library, Tokyo.*

and his heir. In the *ohiroma* in the Hommaru Compound of Edo Castle (Fig. 92), the audience suite was divided into a *jodan,* a *chudan,* and a *gedan* by the same devices used in the *ohiroma* of Nijo Castle. For each level there was a fixed seating arrangement based on the rank of the visiting daimyos, as well as a precise location in which gifts were to be placed.

## ENTERTAINMENT ETIQUETTE

During the Edo period, it was not long before a daimyo's activities, whether carried out in Edo Castle or in his own castle, began to consist largely of prescribed ceremonies that had to be performed at a moment's notice. Even the experienced daimyo found the involved formalities somewhat difficult to handle. Most important among the various ceremonies was the series of succession ceremonies, occasioned by a

shogun's retirement or death, in which the next ruler received confirmation of his right to rule from the emperor. But on any occasion reception of the imperial messenger was not easy. Customarily, several daimyos were assigned the task.

Protocol for imperial receptions did not take the form of a written directive, and to execute such an important task with as little trouble as possible, the daimyo had either to borrow the personal memos of the man previously assigned the task or turn to the masters of court ceremony. The famous sword-brandishing incident of the spring of 1701, known to later generations through the story *Chushingura,* or The Forty-seven Ronin, revolved largely around the difficulties involved with the etiquette proper to ceremonies. Asano Naganori (1667–1701), the daimyo assigned to one such reception, turned to master of ceremonies Kira Yoshinaka Kozuke-nosuke for instruction. Kira, because he felt the

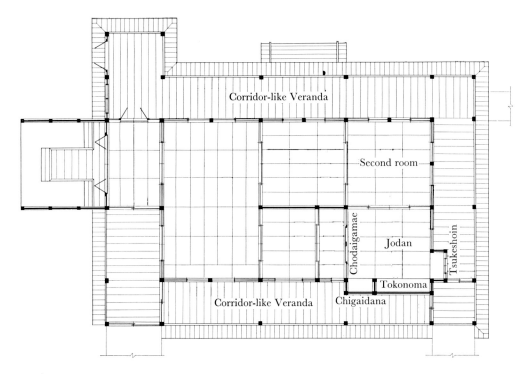

Corridor-like Veranda

Second room

Chodaigamae

Jodan

Tsukeshoin

Tokonoma

Corridor-like Veranda

Chigaidana

*73. Floor plan of audience suite built in 1619 in the Imperial Palace Empress's Palace, according to specifications in documents in the collection of the Imperial Household Agency.*

gratuity he received from Asano was insufficient, not only refused to furnish him with adequate information but also humiliated him. Asano drew his sword and wounded Kira, and for this offense Asano was forced to commit ritual suicide, *seppuku*.

Breaking or being ignorant of customs often caused political disturbances; furthermore, not acting in accordance with etiquette was considered a terrible disgrace. The daimyos therefore recorded protocol for as many of these official ceremonies as they could recall and exchanged memos. Many of these documents have been found among the papers they left.

One example is "How to Serve in the *Jodan* During the First Noh Chanting of the Year; with Illustrations" (Fig. 71), a memorandum that Hotta, the titular governor of Ise Province (in present-day Mie Prefecture), copied from notes borrowed

in 1836 from the titular governor of Chikuzen Province (in present-day Fukuoka Prefecture). One portion of the memorandum says: "On December 28, 1835, Hayashi, Titular Governor of Higo Province, informed the supervisors of court ceremony—Toda, Titular Governor of Awa Province, Toda, Titular Governor of Bitchu Province, and Takai, Titular Governor of Tajima Province— that since the number of occasions to serve had increased lately, they should prepare themselves as best they could in order to be able to execute the assignment smoothly." The memorandum is illustrated to show the procedures and the precise seating to be used when serving the *Sanke*, or Three Houses (the shogun's closest relatives), on the occasion of the New Year reception on the third of January in 1783, 1784, 1785, 1786, and 1834.

In the instructions for serving the shogun as a

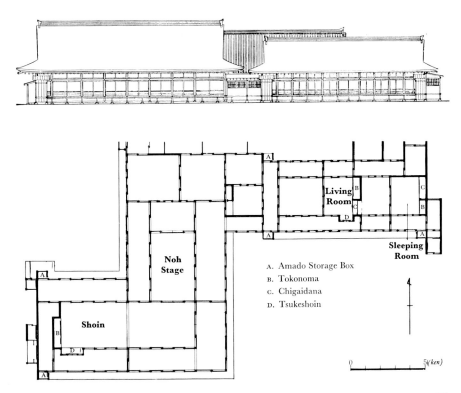

Labels on floor plan:

**Living Room**

**Sleeping Room**

**Noh Stage**

A. Amado Storage Box
B. Tokonoma
C. Chigaidana
D. Tsukeshoin

**Shoin**

0       5 (ken)

*74. Floor plan and elevation of* shoin, *living room, and sleeping room of the Datè residence in Edo in 1657.*

storyteller, for instance, it is recorded that the chief councilor should sit on the third tatami from the shogun, the deputy councilor and the general on the fourth, and the lieutenant-general on the fifth. Documents of the Asano family in Hiroshima and the Ikeda family in Okayama included memoranda recording the procedures followed in Edo Castle on such occasions as, for example, when the Korean ambassador met with the shogun, when the daimyos offered the shogun their New Year greetings, and when the shogun greeted the daimyos before and after viewing a Noh drama. These documents and memoranda show clearly the exacting attention given to status differences.

The annual functions and various ceremonial entertainments presented in the Edo Castle Hommaru Compound *ohiroma* are recorded in *The Record of Tokugawa Manners,* edited by the daimyos Datè Muneshiro, Matsudaira Yoshinaga, and Ikeda Shigemasa in 1881 by order of Emperor Meiji. In this document the item "The Ceremony on the First Day of the Year" reads: "*Gozanoma:* shogun takes his seat in the *jodan;* heir takes his seat in the *jodan;* a list of swords is placed on the second tatami near the outer side of the *jodan.* The *Sankyo* [or Three Lords, relatives of the Tokugawas whose rank was below only that of the *Sanke*] individually place lists of swords on the second tatami of the *gedan,* bow outside the threshold, and take seats on the left side of the *gedan. Shiroshoin:* shogun and heir take seats in the *jodan.* The *Sanke,* with the daimyo of Kaga and others, appear with lists of swords. They bow in the *gedan* and take seats on the left side. They drink a cup of sakè and a bowl of soup, and clothing is presented to them. [Each daimyo receives gifts in return for the swords pre-

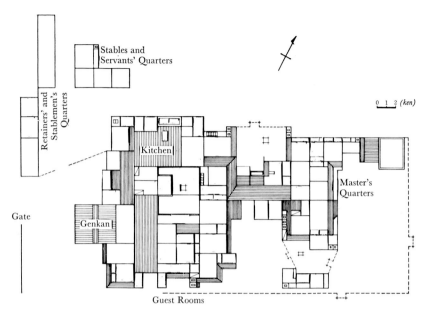

Stables and Servants' Quarters

Retainers' and Stablemen's Quarters

0 1 2 *(ken)*

Kitchen

Master's Quarters

Gate

Genkan

Guest Rooms

*75. Floor plan of residence of Nishio Hayato, retainer of the Maeda clan, about 1760, according to documents in Kanazawa City Public Library.*

sented to the shogun. The clothing is that which the shogun himself once used.] Guests retire to the adjoining room. Matsudaira, Titular Governor of Sanuki Province, and others appear with lists of swords and all bow individually on the threshold or outside the threshold, depending on their ranks. *Ohiroma:* shogun and heir enter the *gedan. Fudai* [hereditary vassals] and the *tozama* [lords who became vassals only after 1600] having land valued at more than 10,000 *koku* all bow. Shogun and heir take seats in the *jodan.* Matsudaira, Titular Governor of Izumi Province, and other daimyos each receive drinks and clothing. Retainers having land valued at more than 10,000 *koku* bow. Clothing is presented to them.''

Under the rule of Tokugawa Ieyasu, a clear hierarchy of social ranks was set forth, and status differences between the Tokugawa shogun and the daimyos and among the various daimyos were firmly established. By the time Tokugawa Iemitsu

(1604–51) became ruler in 1623, status differences had become rigid. The relationship between the Tokugawas and the Maeda family of Kaga Province (present-day Ishikawa Prefecture), the most powerful daimyo family at the beginning of Tokugawa rule, is a good illustration of the changing hierarchy. Maeda Toshiie first served under Oda Nobunaga; but after that leader was assassinated at Kyoto's Honno-ji temple, Toshiie became one of the most important vassals of Toyotomi Hideyoshi in the years that Hideyoshi was gaining military hegemony. Tokugawa Ieyasu, who also began as an ally of Nobunaga, joined forces with Hideyoshi. Under Hideyoshi's leadership, Toshiie and Ieyasu served as generals and thus in a sense were colleagues. As the Tokugawas grew more powerful, however, they restricted the Maedas' influence to their Kaga domain, which had a rice yield of one million *koku* (about five million bushels). The size of this holding distinguished the Maeda family as

76. *Eastern frontage of guest hall of Kojo-in;* chumon *is to left of* karahafu-*gabled entrance. 1601. Onjo-in temple, Otsu, Shiga Prefecture. (See also Figure 90.)*

77. *Corridor-like veranda, veranda, and* chumon *(at rear) of guest hall of Kangaku-in. 1600. Onjo-ji temple, Otsu, Shiga Prefecture. (See also Figures 78, 141, 142.)*

*78. Tokonoma of main room in guest hall of Kangaku-in. 1600. Onjo-ji temple, Otsu, Shiga Prefecture. (See also Figures 77, 141, 142.)*

*82. Elaborate* chigaidana *in main room of guest hall in the middle garden of Shugaku-in Detached Palace. Completed 1677; moved to present site after 1682. Kyoto. (See also Figure 103.)*

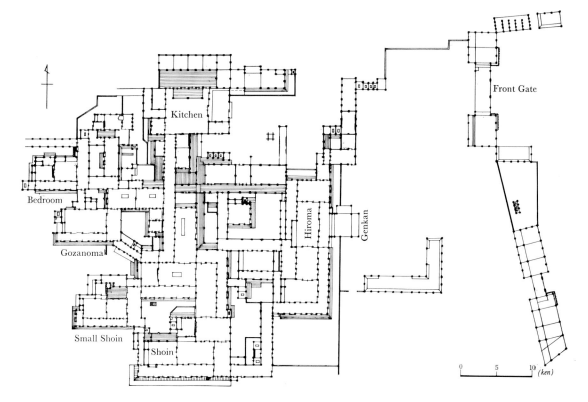

Labels on plan: Kitchen, Front Gate, Bedroom, Hiroma, Genkan, Gozanoma, Small Shoin, Shoin

0    5    10 (ken)

*83. Ground plan of the Datè residence built in Edo in 1658, according to specifications in documents in the collection of the Datè family.*

having the largest rice yield among all the daimyos.

Although the Maedas received no preferential treatment under Tokugawa rule, they did have the honor of being visited by the Tokugawas. *The Description of the Shogunal Visits in 1629,* owned by the Maeda family, records the visit of the third shogun, Iemitsu, on April 26 and that of the retired shogun, Hidetada, on April 29, 1629. A copy of this document is deposited with the Kanazawa City Library. The document says: "Drinks at the *kuroshoin* [informal *shoin*]. At the *shoin,* a 7-5-3 banquet [seven courses, followed by five courses, then by three]. At the *kuroshoin,* shogunal endowments and gifts to the shogun. A Noh performance at the *ohiroma.* In the *kuroshoin,* drinks."

From the documents in Figure 72, we know that at this time there were three pictures hanging in the tokonoma of the *ohiroma:* the first depicting a dragon, the second depicting a Chinese priest, and the third, a tiger. To the left of these pictures, on the wooden floor of the tokonoma, was a formal floral arrangement with pine branches, to the right was a floral arrangement with bamboo, and between these two arrangements were a golden incense container and an incense burner shaped like a tortoise. The *chigaidana* adjoining the tokonoma were decorated with an incense burner, a lacquered container inlaid with a chrysanthemum and water design, and an ornamental food case coated with more than a hundred layers of lacquer. Above the *tsukeshoin* hung a bell; and on the broad windowsill were an inkstone, a water container, a Korean bowl for cleaning brushes, and other objects.

In the *jodan* itself there was an additional tatami

*84. Garden of the Rikugi-en villa. Eighteenth century. Tokyo.*

upon which was placed a cushion made of golden brocade, much the same arrangement as seen in Figure 109. There was also a lacquered and inlaid sword rack. The *gedan* also had additional tatami, a cushion, and a sword rack of red sandalwood. As for information on how the *jodan* and *gedan* were used, we have the *Record of the Taiko* [Hideyoshi] *and Shogunal Visits*, owned by the Kanazawa City Library. The entry recording Hidetada's visit to Maeda Toshimitsu's residence on May 13, 1617, tells us: "The shogun came . . . to the *shoin* . . . as the dinner in his honor was being brought in; he took his seat in the *jodan*, and Toshimitsu, Titular Governor of Chikuzen, took his seat in the *gedan*." On this occasion both the shogun and Toshimitsu were seated upon an additional tatami that had been placed in their respective rooms.

DAIMYO RESIDENCES     Although only a few residential buildings dating from the Edo period remain today, plans of Edo Castle and many of the daimyos' residences exist. The principal buildings in these residences faced gardens, as did the buildings in the Ninomaru, or Second, Compound of Nijo Castle. As illustrated in the foldout facing page 72, inside the main gate of a typical warrior residence was a small, flat area beyond which was the *kurumayose* (carriage entrance) or the *genkan* with a *shikidai* (a room just inside the *genkan* for retainers to wait in). It was at the *kurumayose* or *genkan* that the palanquin of the visitor rested upon arrival. Inside the entrance was a large room with a tokonoma, which was used as a waiting room. Behind the *genkan* and connected to it by a short corridor was the large *shoin*, the major reception building in the *shoin* style. Behind this and also connected by a short corridor was the small *shoin* (used for meeting guests), which on formal occasions became a banquet room. Farther back was the inner *shoin*, where the master lived during the day. In a shogun's residence this was the building in which he administered the affairs of state, met high officials, and held more intimate receptions and meetings. These administrators used another building located nearby to rest in; it was in this same building that the sleeping quarters for the shogun were located.

When the Noh drama became an indispensable part of formal entertainment and was made the official entertainment of the Tokugawa government, the stage erected in a warrior's garden in front of the major reception building became a

*85. The Lady's Gate of the Maeda residence in Edo, now known as the Red Gate on Tokyo University Campus. 1827. Tokyo.*

permanent structure. Other principal structures of the warrior's residence included a number of service buildings, a large kitchen with the living quarters for servants, and the various buildings for the mistress of the house. The residences of lower-ranking warriors were smaller in scale, and the most important rooms were the reception room and the master's living quarters.

A daimyo's residence in Edo was usually surrounded by small, thickly plastered row houses with a common roof where his retainers lived. During earlier periods there were large gardens in front of all the daimyo's important buildings, as can still be seen in Nijo Castle (Fig. 112 and foldout following page 128); but as the number of buildings increased, the gardens became smaller until the garden in front of the inner *shoin* was the only one remaining. When a large garden was desired, it was made in the grounds of a suburban villa that had space enough for a garden on a grand scale. The Koraku-en in Tokyo, for example, was once the garden of the Mito family; and the Rikugi-en (Fig. 84), also in Tokyo, was originally the garden that Yanagisawa Yoshiyasu (1658–1714), the special aide and protégé of the fifth Tokugawa shogun, Tsunayoshi, built at his villa. Among large gardens

in existence today that were built by daimyos in their domains are Suizen-ji Park in Kumamoto, the Koraku-en in Okayama, the Ritsurin-en in Takamatsu, the Kenroku-en in Kanazawa, and the Kairaku-en in Mito.

In warrior residences the major reception building in the *shoin* style (the large *shoin*) in most cases faced south, with the ridges of its roof lying in an east-west direction. There were two or three rooms varying from eight to thirty mats in area built in a row in an east-west direction and surrounded by broad corridor-like verandas. Occasionally, the veranda at the rear was omitted, but the side facing the front garden normally had a veranda one or two *ken* wide (roughly two or four meters). The innermost room, the room farthest from the entrance, had a raised floor fifteen to twenty centimeters higher than the floors of the other rooms.

In a large *shoin* building the audience suite typically had three connected rooms, each of a different elevation. The room with the lowest elevation is called the *gedan;* the room with the middle elevation is the *chudan;* and the *jodan* of former times, which was then actually a dais, evolved into the room with the highest elevation, which retains the name *jodan.* The relationships of these rooms can

88. The shinden of Daikaku-ji temple. 1619; moved to present site c. 1650. Kyoto.

the building and slide out of the way into built-in storage boxes when not in use, thus allowing sunlight to stream into the rooms through the wainscoted *shoji*.

In the Edo residences of daimyos, the means of conveying one's prestige to the masses were limited to the front gate and the large gables. In the very early Edo period the daimyos, who were required to maintain residences in Edo, competed in building the most magnificent gates. One of the best known is the gate of the residence of Kato Kiyomasa, the daimyo of Higo Province (present-day Kumamoto Prefecture), whose Kumamoto Castle we have discussed. Laden with lively and attractive golden carvings, Kiyomasa's gate was named the Gate of Entrancing Brilliance. Kora Konen, head carpentry supervisor in Edo for the Tokugawa government, recorded the following about the gates of the residence that belonged to

Matsudaira Tadamasa (1597–1645), the titular governor of Iyo Province (present-day Ehime Prefecture): "The gate used for receiving the shogun is a large one with a *karahafu*-gabled roof. It is decorated with carvings of dragons, lions, and geometrical designs. The door panels have carvings of Taoist gods, and carvings also adorn the bolts. The entire structure is covered with glittering gold foil. The front gate, which has a hipped roof, is also entirely gilded and decorated with carvings of lions and dragons."

In an effort to stabilize the political system, the Tokugawa government established numerous ranks. One measure of samurai status was the stipend they received, which was paid in *koku* (about five bushels) of rice. Ostentation was restrained as the government set restrictions forbidding extravagance. However, each warrior was strictly required to indicate his status by means of

89. *Tokonoma and* chigaidana *in main room of guest hall of Kanchi-in. 1605. To-ji temple, Kyoto. (See also Figure 143.)*

the front gate of his residence. This was done in accordance with government restrictions: a warrior was not allowed to have a gate style assigned to a rank either higher or lower than his own.

In Edo, for example, according to his rank a daimyo's residence had to have one of the following entrances: a daimyo ruling an entire province—an entrance gate with a gabled or a hipped-and-gabled roof and on each side of the gate a guardhouse with a *karahafu*-gabled roof, the lower half of all walls covered with stone or clay tiles; a daimyo receiving a stipend of more than 100,000 *koku*—a *nagayamon* (literally, "long-house gate," actually an entrance gate without flaring eaves) and at each side a guardhouse with a *karahafu*-gabled roof; a daimyo who had been a retainer of the Tokugawas before 1600, when the first Tokugawa shogun came to power, and receiving more than 50,000 *koku* but less than 100,000 *koku*—a *nagayamon* with guard-

houses with slanting roofs on each side; a daimyo made a retainer after 1600 and receiving more than 50,000 *koku*—a *nagayamon* and only one guardhouse with a gabled roof; a daimyo receiving more than 30,000 *koku*—a *nagayamon* and only one guardhouse with a slanting roof; a daimyo receiving more than 10,000 *koku* but less than 30,000 *koku*—a *nagayamon* with a latticed window on each side.

In addition, a daimyo who married a shogun's daughter was required to erect a red gate in front of her quarters. He took good care of this gate, knowing full well that it added to his prestige. Akamon (Fig. 85), the Red Gate on the campus of Tokyo University, was built in 1827 by Maeda Nariyasu, of the thirteenth generation of the Maeda daimyo family of Kaga Province, as part of the preparations for his marriage to Princess Yo, one of the daughters of the eleventh Tokugawa shogun, Ienari.

# CHAPTER THREE

—— • ——

# Development of the Shoin Style

ROOM
ARRANGEMENT
During the sixteenth and the beginning of the seventeenth centuries, all daily indoor activities in Japan were usually performed in one central building. Since the entertainment of guests and the holding of audiences, various games, and such contests as tea identifying gradually increased during this period and became an important part of an aristocrat's public activities, some upper-class residences had buildings used mainly for verse writing and other leisure activities, residential quarters (*tsune no gosho*) separate from the main building, and a main building used exclusively for ceremonies and formal audiences.

In most residences, however, daily activities were performed in the central building of the compound. This was partly due to the fact that both the military, holding actual power with the Ashikaga shogun as the figurehead, and the aristocrats, who relied on their estates for their livelihood, were economically exhausted after the Onin Civil War (1467–77) and could no longer afford residences on a large scale. Let us trace the process through which the floor plans commonly used during the middle ages, as typified by those used in the Gyoko Goten (the temporary palace built in Nijo Castle for the emperor) and those used in the buildings in the *shuden* style (that is, with both a *chumon* and a *kuru-mayose*), developed into a plan with a single-row arrangement of rooms.

At the beginning of the Edo period, the floor plan commonly used until then began to change. Many buildings included rooms that by this time had lost their original function. The living room and the *chodai* (sleeping alcove), usually located next to the main room of the audience suite, were no longer needed when separate buildings with residential quarters were built. For example, one of the buildings of the Konoe residence in Kyoto had a long corridor to the inner gate (as had been traditional during the Heian period); actually the floor plan resembled that of the Gyoko Goten (see foldout opposite page 128) and had a main room with a wooden-floored tokonoma and *chigaidana* like those in the middle *jodan* of the Gyoko Goten. However, the tokonoma and *chigaidana* of the main and second rooms of the Konoe residence were on the common wall between the rooms; and there were neither *chodai* nor *chodaigamae,* since separate residential quarters had already been set up elsewhere.

Eventually a *chodai*, and the space that the living room once occupied, was incorporated into the audience suite. Both patterns resulted in the L-shaped arrangement of rooms that was commonly used in the structures built during the Edo period. The latter pattern appears in the *tozamurai*, the *kuroshoin*, and the *shiroshoin* in the Ninomaru Compound of Nijo Castle and in the Kojo-in guest hall located in the grounds of Onjo-ji temple in Shiga Prefecture. The most important room of the Kojo-in guest hall (Fig. 90) not only is equipped

*90. Tokonoma and* chigaidana *in main room of guest hall of Kojo-in. 1601. Onjo-ji temple, Otsu, Shiga Prefecture. (See also Figure 76.)*

with a tokonoma and *chigaidana* but also has *chodaigamae* that lead neither to a sleeping alcove, as do those in the guest hall of the Kanchi-in subtemple in the grounds of To-ji temple in Kyoto, nor to a waiting room, as do those in the *ohiroma* in the Ninomaru Compound of Nijo Castle.

It is not clear why *chodaigamae* were used in the *shoin*-style room of a temple, but since they are also found in Kanchi-in the doors were obviously not without some function in temple architecture. The introduction of *chodaigamae* in the Kojo-in guest hall might be explained by the fact that Yamaoka Doami, who is said to have built the guest hall as a patron, came from a warrior family. Doors that were purely decorative and did not lead to a *chodai* were also used in structures of a much larger scale, such as in the *ohiroma* in the Juraku-dai castle-palace in Kyoto, built during the Tensho era (1573–92), the *ohiroma* in the Hommaru Compound

of Nagoya Castle, the *ohiroma* in the castle the daimyo Datè Masamune built in 1610 in Sendai, and the *ohiroma* of Sasayama Castle in Tamba, which was built in 1609. These *ohiroma* also had a triple row of rooms, a *chumon*, and a *karahafu* gable at the eaves of the façade.

There are many examples of the L-shaped arrangement in *ohiroma*: the *ohiroma* cited in one of the *Shomei* volumes; those pictured in the documents owned by the Sakagami family, which were prepared during the Keicho era (1596–1615); the *ohiroma* belonging to the daimyo of Owari Province, described in *Notes of the Kishigami Family*, written in 1628; and the *ohiroma* in the Hommaru Compound of Nagoya Castle, built in the Keicho era. Other examples of *ohiroma* in this style dating from the Kan'ei era (1624–44) were built in Osaka Castle; in the Hommaru Compound of the Nijo Castle complex; in the Hommaru Compound of the

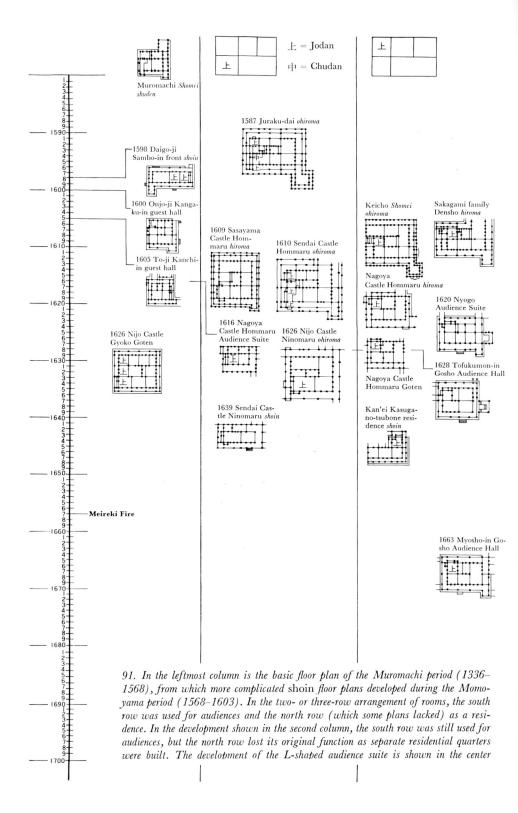

| 上 = Jodan |
| 中 = Chudan |

Muromachi *Shomei shuden*

1587 Juraku-dai *ohiroma*

1598 Daigo-ji Sambo-in front *shoin*

1600 Onjo-ji Kanga-ku-in guest hall

1605 To-ji Kanchi-in guest hall

1609 Sasayama Castle Hommaru *hiroma*

1610 Sendai Castle Hommaru *ohiroma*

Keicho *Shomei ohiroma*

Sakagami family Densho *hiroma*

Nagoya Castle Hommaru *hiroma*

1616 Nagoya Castle Hommaru Audience Suite

1626 Nijo Castle Ninomaru *ohiroma*

1620 Nyogo Audience Suite

1626 Nijo Castle Gyoko Goten

Nagoya Castle Hommaru Goten

1628 Tofukumon-in Gosho Audience Hall

1639 Sendai Castle Ninomaru *shoin*

Kan'ei Kasugano-tsubone residence *shoin*

Meireki Fire

1663 Myosho-in Gosho Audience Hall

91. *In the leftmost column is the basic floor plan of the Muromachi period (1336–1568), from which more complicated shoin floor plans developed during the Momoyama period (1568–1603). In the two- or three-row arrangement of rooms, the south row was used for audiences and the north row (which some plans lacked) as a residence. In the development shown in the second column, the south row was still used for audiences, but the north row lost its original function as separate residential quarters were built. The development of the L-shaped audience suite is shown in the center*

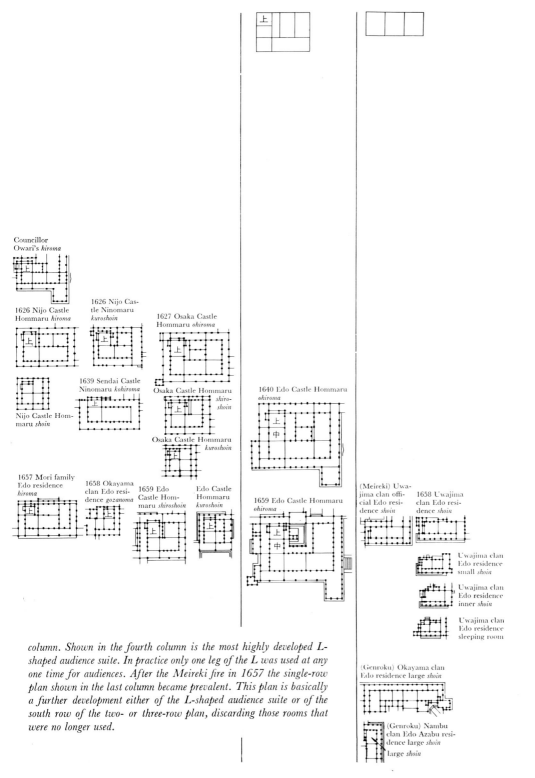

Councillor Owari's *hiroma*

1626 Nijo Castle Hommaru *hiroma*

1626 Nijo Castle Ninomaru *kuroshoin*

1627 Osaka Castle Hommaru *ohiroma*

1639 Sendai Castle Ninomaru *kohiroma*

Nijo Castle Hommaru *shoin*

Osaka Castle Hommaru *shiroshoin*

Osaka Castle Hommaru *kuroshoin*

1640 Edo Castle Hommaru *ohiroma*

1657 Mori family Edo residence *hiroma*

1658 Okayama clan Edo residence *gozanoma*

1659 Edo Castle Hommaru *shiroshoin*

Edo Castle Hommaru *kuroshoin*

1659 Edo Castle Hommaru *ohiroma*

(Meireki) Uwajima clan official Edo residence *shoin*

1658 Uwajima clan Edo residence *shoin*

Uwajima clan Edo residence small *shoin*

Uwajima clan Edo residence inner *shoin*

Uwajima clan Edo residence sleeping room

(Genroku) Okayama clan Edo residence large *shoin*

(Genroku) Nambu clan Edo Azabu residence large *shoin*

large *shoin*

*column. Shown in the fourth column is the most highly developed L-shaped audience suite. In practice only one leg of the L was used at any one time for audiences. After the Meireki fire in 1657 the single-row plan shown in the last column became prevalent. This plan is basically a further development either of the L-shaped audience suite or of the south row of the two- or three-row plan, discarding those rooms that were no longer used.*

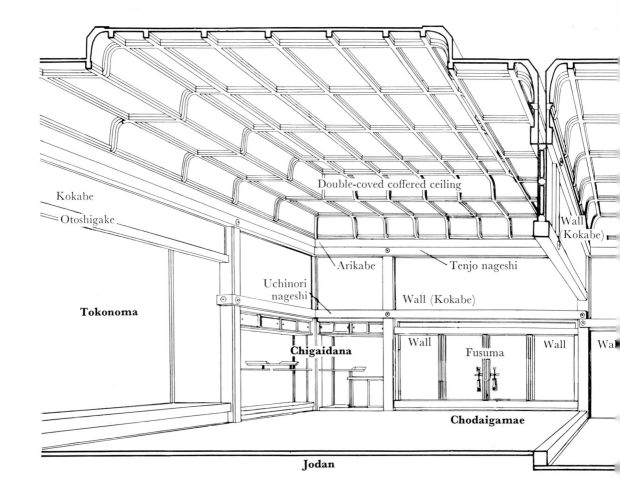

Kokabe

Otoshigake

Double-coved coffered ceiling

Wall (Kokabe)

Arikabe　　　　Tenjo nageshi

Uchinori
nageshi

Wall (Kokabe)

**Tokonoma**

Wall　　　　　Wall　　　Wa

**Chigaidana**

Fusuma

**Chodaigamae**

**Jodan**

Sumpu Castle complex in Shizuoka Prefecture; in the audience chamber of the Empress's Palace, Kyoto; and in the outer and inner audience chambers of the Tofukumon-in Palace, Kyoto. The L-shaped audience suite was the first arrangement of rooms to develop after separate living quarters were built.

The structures characterized by rooms arranged in double or triple rows evolved in two directions. One development was reflected in the *ohiroma* in the Hommaru Compound of Edo castle. This *ohiroma*, built in 1640, had two rows of rooms placed so that each row formed one leg of a five-room L-shape.

One row, used for formal receptions, as at New Year or when a new shogun was installed, consisted of three rooms (Fig. 92): the *jodan*, which was the main room in the row and had a tokonoma, *chigaidana*, a *tsukeshoin*, and *chodaigamae;* the *chudan;* and the *gedan*. The shogun's status was expressed by his sitting in the most elevated section, the *jodan*, while the various statuses of the daimyos were indicated by their being seated at various distances from the shogun and on different floor levels. This expression of status made the room arrangement of the *ohiroma* complex. The other row of rooms, which had the *gedan* of the first row as its most important

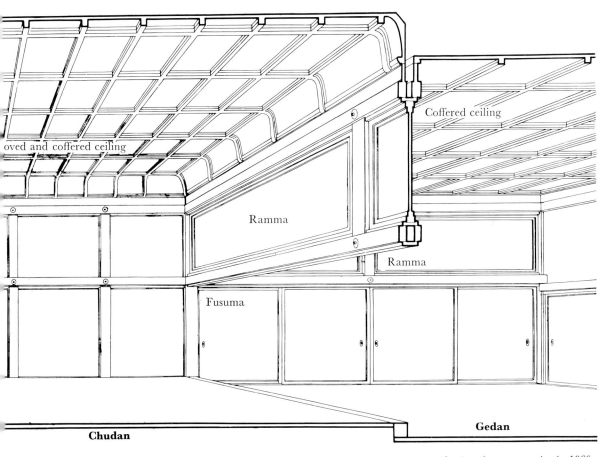

Coffered ceiling

oved and coffered ceiling

Ramma

Ramma

Fusuma

Chudan

Gedan

92. *Cross section of* ohiroma *in Hommaru Compound of Edo Castle, according to specifications for reconstruction in 1860.*

room, was used when the shogun had to meet a group of daimyos on ceremonial occasions.

Since a separate structure had been built for residential purposes, there was no need for any rooms in the *shoin* other than those for holding audiences. Thus the other structural development occurred when certain rooms were simply discarded as need for them decreased, resulting in two or three rooms arranged in a single row. One of the earlier examples of this arrangement is the front *shoin* of Sambo-in (Figs. 95, 102), a subtemple in the grounds of the Daigo-ji temple in Kyoto. This *shoin* was built in 1598 and had the *shuden*-style *chumon*

and a *kurumayose* decorated with a *karahafu* gable.

When an entire compound was relatively small, all quarters were located in a single building; two rows of rooms were placed north and south of each other in that building—one for giving audiences and the other for residential purposes. A typical example of this double-row structure can be seen in the guest hall of Kanchi-in, in which the audience suite (Fig. 89) consists of two rooms on the south side with a living room and a *chodai* on the north side. The Imperial Palace and temple complexes related to imperial families had separate buildings for holding audiences and for residential purposes.

*93. Tokonoma of great* jodan *and* chigaidana *and* tsukeshoin *of small* jodan *in audience suite of Nishi Hongan-ji temple. Seventeenth century. Kyoto. (See also Figures 97, 154, 155.)*

But since the building with the residential quarters was often used for audiences, it usually had an audience suite built on its south side and a living room and a *chodai* on the north side.

Some of the structures built on a larger scale had rooms—used for informal meetings and games—to the north of the living room and the *chodai*. The result was a triple-row structure like that which can be found in the Kangaku-in guest hall. Of the three rows comprising this guest hall, the south row consists of rooms used for holding audiences. The only room decorations in the main part of the audience suite (Fig. 78) are a large tokonoma and a painting in brilliant colors on a gold ground, attributed to the artist Kano Mitsunobu (1561–1608), a son of Eitoku, who had decorated Azuchi Castle. The living room (Fig. 141), directly to the north of the main room, has a tokonoma, a *tsukeshoin*, and paintings on the walls done in soft ink. Its atmos-

phere is entirely different from that of the audience suite. The bedroom, to the east of the living room, unlike the one in the guest hall of Kanchi-in, has *fusuma* instead of fixed walls and gives the impression of being very open. In fact, only the mosquito-net hooks remaining on the four corner pillars indicate that it was once used as a bedroom.

But the single-row arrangement became the basis of the *shoin* structure and was widely adopted after the great Meireki fire of 1657. After this fire, not only was the *shoin* style with a single-row structure, devoid of useless rooms, widely adopted for most audience halls but the architectural features commonly employed during the middle ages (such as the *chumon* and the *kurumayose*) were finally discarded. Plans of warrior residences built in Edo after the Meireki fire still remain with the Ikeda family in Okayama and the Datè family in Uwajima and with other families whose ancestors were

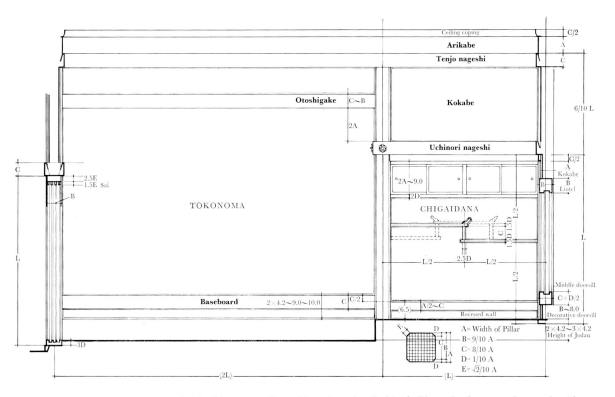

Labels in figure: Ceiling coping, Arikabe, Tenjo nageshi, C/2, C, Otoshigake, C~B, Kokabe, 6/10 L, 2A, Uchinori nageshi, C/2, A, Kokabe, B, Lintel, 2.5E, 1.5E Sai, °2A~9.0, 2D, CHIGAIDANA, C, 1.5D 1.5D, L/2, TOKONOMA, L/2, 2.5D, L/2, L, L/2, Middle doorsill, C+D/2, B~8.0, Decorative doorsill, Baseboard, 2×4.2~9.0~10.0, C, C/2, (6.5), A/2~C, Recessed wall, 2×4.2~3×4.2 Height of Jodan, 3D, D, A=Width of Pillar, B=9/10 A, C=8/10 A, D=1/10 A, E=√2/10 A, (2L), (L)

*94. Specifications for tokonoma and* chigaidana *according to* kiwari, *as described in the* Shomei *volume on palaces and residences.*

daimyos. One example of a single-row *shoin* is the one in the Datès' Edo residence (Figs. 74, 83), which was built immediately after the fire and had two rooms arranged in one row, unlike structures in earlier architectural styles, which had rooms arranged in two or three rows. However, we should keep in mind that not all structures built during the early Edo period had audience suites whose rooms were arranged in a single row, nor was the *chumon* of the *shuden* style always discarded.

## TRADITIONAL DESIGN STANDARDS

In the early Edo period, the techniques that were prescribed for designing residences of warriors were known as *kiwari jutsu*, or the art of determining construction ratios. The calculation used for determining the measurements used in construction was based upon the thickness of the structural pillars and the distance between two pillars. Among the existing and best-organized books on *kiwari jutsu*, the oldest is *Shomei*, which has been mentioned before. It consists of five volumes, each devoted to a single subject: palaces and residences, gates, shrines, temples, and towers. The set, a compilation of descriptions of actual buildings, was intended to provide exacting standards of design. In actual application, however, these standards were not strictly followed but were used instead as general references.

From descriptions in the *Shomei* volume on residences, it is possible to reconstruct the central quarters of a warrior's residence around 1608. From the descriptions of the interior structures and the drawing appended to the volume, we know that the most important room of the residence was equipped with a tokonoma almost four meters wide and, adjoining it, *chigaidana* half that size.

In the days when architectural construction was

95. *Tokonoma and* chigaidana *in front* shoin *of Sambo-in. 1598. Daigo-ji temple, Kyoto. (See also Figure 102.)*

largely based on tradition and structural restrictions carried considerable weight, it was nearly impossible to make substantial changes in the size of the principal elements, such as the pillars and beams, unless they were used in small structures, such as tearooms. Interior elements, such as the tokonoma and the *chigaidana,* were the only parts of the building that played no major role in terms of overall structure but were genuinely important in terms of design.

The location of the *otoshigake* (the beam at the bottom of a *kokabe,* or partial wall, between rooms or between the tokonoma alcove and the room it is part of) above the tokonoma became the principal factor in effecting changes in the design of the tokonoma. As shown in Figure 94, the *Shomei* volume on residences notes that between the bottom edge of the *otoshigake* and the top edge of the *uchinori nageshi* (the connecting decorative band or half-beam that

runs between two pillars at the bottom of a *kokabe* that is part of a functional wall; it is analogous to the *otoshigake*) above the adjoining *chigaidana* there should be a space that is equal to twice the thickness of the pillars in the building.

In Edo Castle, the *otoshigake* above the various tokonomas are, in most cases, much closer to the *uchinori nageshi* above the *chigaidana* than to the *tenjo nageshi* (the band or half-beam at the top of the *kokabe*), and at the highest elevation the *otoshigake* reached a point midway between these two beams. However, in Osaka and Nijo castles, the *otoshigake* are closer to the *tenjo nageshi* than to the *uchinori nageshi* above the *chigaidana*. Consequently, the *otoshigake* in Edo Castle, shown in Figure 92, looks conspicuously lower than those of the other two castles.

In all three castles, the distance between the *otoshigake* and the *uchinori nageshi* above the *chigai-*

*96. Tokonoma,* chigaidana, *and L-shaped* jodan *in main room of* shiroshoin *of Nishi Hongan-ji temple;* tsukeshoin *and* chodai-gamae *are just visible on left and right. Seventeenth century. Kyoto. (See also Figures 98, 154, 156.)*

*97 (overleaf). Tokonoma and* jodan *of audience suite of Nishi Hongan-ji temple. To far right,* ▷ *behind screened fan-shaped window, is the small* jodan, *raised an additional level above the great* jodan. *Seventeenth century. Kyoto. (See also Figures 93, 154, 155.)*

*100. Aerial view of Nijo Castle Ninomaru Palace: from left to right,* kuroshoin, ohiroma, shikidai, *and* tozamurai, *with* kurumayose *in front. Barely visible behind the* kuroshoin *is roof of* shiroshoin; *roof of kitchen is visible behind the* tozamurai. *1626. Kyoto. (See also Figure 112.)*

*101.* Karahafu *gable and openwork frieze of* kurumayose *of the Ninomaru Palace in Nijo Castle; gable of* tozamurai *is visible in background. 1626. Kyoto. (See also Figures 116, 117.)*

*102. Front* shoin *of Sambo-in. 1598. Daigo-ji temple, Kyoto. (See also Figure 95.)*

*dana* is greater than twice the thickness of the structural pillars, thus far from meeting the standard set forth in *Shomei,* although Edo Castle does follow the standard more closely than the others. Plans, dated 1860, depicting the *otoshigake* in Edo Castle and the plans for the *ohiroma* built in the Edo Castle Hommaru Compound in 1640 show the *otoshigake* midway between the *uchinori nageshi* and the *tenjo nageshi.*

In the guest hall of the Kita-in temple (Fig. 80) in Saitama Prefecture, which is said to have been moved from Edo Castle in 1638, the *otoshigake* is closer to the *uchinori nageshi.* However, in the Kansai area, which was under the control of the Nakai family of carpentry supervisors, the *otoshigake* are situated relatively high, for example, in Osaka and Nijo castles and all other formal structures built in this area. In temple *shoin,* the *otoshigake* are lo-

cated quite near the *tenjo nageshi.* In the audience suite of the Nishi Hongan-ji temple (Fig. 93), the tokonoma, almost six meters wide, provides an extreme example: the *otoshigake* lies adjacent to the *tenjo nageshi,* so that there is no wall whatsoever between these two beams.

In the *ohiroma* in the Ninomaru Compound of Nijo Castle, the *kokabe* between the *jodan* and the *gedan* is so small that the two rooms look like one (Fig. 99). But in the *ohiroma* in the Hommaru Compound of Edo Castle (Fig. 92), the *kokabe* between the *jodan* and the *chudan* extends farther down from the ceiling, and the *otoshigake* under the *kokabe* that is between the *chudan* and the *gedan* is actually a lintel. These *kokabe* and *otoshigake* effectively separate the three rooms into independent parts while still joining them into one hall.

In the early Edo period, the powerful Nakai

| | A | C | | A | C |
|---|---|---|---|---|---|
| Veranda post | 3.6 | 3.6 | Base rafter width | 1.82 | 1.8 |
| Veranda support | ×1.9 | ×1.8 | Batten depth | 0.99 | 1.08 |
| Veranda floor thickness | 1.09 | 1.13 | Batten width | 1.42 | 1.44 |
| Veranda width | 37.9 | | Eaves width | 64.7 | 65.0 |
| Ground to veranda | 16.3 | | Roof pitch | 6.8 | |
| Veranda *nageshi* | 2.31 | | Pillars | 4.0 | 4.0 (assumed) |
| Veranda height | 71.2 | | Trimmed pillars | 3.6 | 3.6 |
| Doorsill depth | 1.88 | 1.8 | Lintel depth | 1.72 | 1.8 |
| Lintel depth | 1.42 | | *Sai* depth | 0.89 | 0.9 |
| Veranda pillars | 4.52 | 4.5 | Height to *uchinori* | 60.0 | 60.0 |
| *Kokabe* height | 34.1 | 34.0 | *Uchinori nageshi* depth | 3.7 | 3.8 |
| Ridgepole depth | 11.9 | 12.0 | *Tenjo nageshi* depth | 3.8 | 3.8 |
| Base rafter depth | 2.15 | 2.16 | Ceiling ribs | 1.82 | 1.8 |

103 (above). Tokonoma and elaborate chigaidana *in main room of guest hall in middle garden of Shugaku-in Detached Palace. Completed 1677; moved to present site after 1682. Kyoto. (See also Figure 82.)*

104. *Measurements of the audience suite in the guest hall in the middle garden of Shugaku-in Detached Palace in Kyoto. All measurements are given in sun, about 1.19 inches. Column A measurements are actual; column C measurements are calculated from records.*

*105.* Jodan *in small* hojo *of Chion-in; note additional tatami on floor of* jodan. *1641. Kyoto. (See also Figure 153.)*

family of Kyoto dominated the Kansai area as the head carpentry supervisors in charge of construction undertaken by the Tokugawas. Not only did the family supervise the construction of Sumpu Castle in present-day Shizuoka Prefecture, but its members joined the head carpenters of Edo in building the Hommaru Compound of Edo Castle in 1637, 1640, and 1659.

In contrast, the Edo head carpenters neither participated in the construction of Nijo and Osaka castles nor helped during the two periods when construction work in Kyoto was at its peak: the 1661–63 period, when five imperial palace structures were constructed simultaneously, and the 1673–78 period, when seven imperial structures were constructed in succession. In the 1708–9 period, when palaces for the emperor and two retired emperors were planned in Kyoto, the Edo carpenters attempted to have their head carpenters participate in the projects on the grounds that Nakai

Masatomo was then more than eighty years old. Nakai Masatomo himself objected, so the attempt did not succeed; but this incident demonstrates the confidence the Kansai carpenters had in their tradition and authority as against those of the newly established carpenters of Edo.

That authority notwithstanding, many of the books on *kiwari* that were most widely used after the mid-seventeenth century followed the standards used in Edo, and the carpenters of Edo in effect became the ultimate authorities on the subject. The lower position of the *otoshigake* in Edo structures may well have been their attempt to differentiate their style from that of the Kansai area. Figure 104 gives the measurements of various parts of the inner audience suite in the Tofukumon-in Palace, which is now known as the guest hall of the middle garden (Figs. 82, 103) in the grounds of the Shugaku-in Detached Palace in Kyoto.

The measurements of this building, constructed

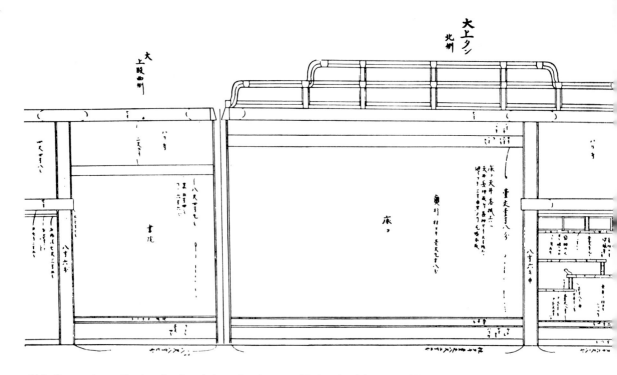

*106. Panoramic specifications for formal decorative elements of* jodan *in* ohiroma *in Hommaru Compound of Osaka Castle. From left to right, elements are the* tsukeshoin, tokonoma, L-shaped *chigaidana, and* chodaigamae. *Executed by Furuhashi c. 1850. Tokyo Institute of Technology. (See also Figure 124.)*

in 1677 by the Nakai family, correspond closely to those given in the *Shomei* volume on residences, indicating that by this time the buildings in Edo and in the Kansai area did not differ greatly. All the existing well-organized and systematic descriptions of *kiwari* are owned by the descendants of such families as the Kora and Heinouchi, head carpentry supervisors of Edo, and by carpentry supervisors whose descendants were local daimyo, such as the Shimizu family in Kaga Province (present-day Ishikawa Prefecture), but they are not to be found among the documents of the more traditional Kansai head carpenters.

During the early Edo period, when the power of the warrior class was at its peak, there were not many such complete *shoin*-style buildings as the *ohiroma* in the Hommaru Compound of Edo Castle, or like those found in the Ninomaru Compound of Nijo Castle, that had all four elements: a tokonoma, chigaidana, a *tsukeshoin,* and *chodaigamae.* The guest hall (Fig. 80) of the Kita-in temple in Saitama Prefecture has a *tokonoma* and *chigaidana* but no *tsukeshoin* or *chodaigamae.* Even the study hall (Fig. 107) of the present Kyoto Imperial Palace has only a tokonoma and *chigaidana.* Adjoining the emperor's private quarters is a building that he ordinarily used for audiences, but the *jodan* room did not have a tokonoma. Often in the residences of the nobility only *chigaidana* were used, since the number and kinds of decorative elements used were quite flexible. In the residences of the warriors, however, the status of the master of the house determined which of the decorative elements were used: persons of the highest rank used all four elements, whereas those of the lowest rank had only the tokonoma.

There was a similar tendency to express status in the use of the mural. The daimyos who had newly risen to power naturally attempted to impress visi-

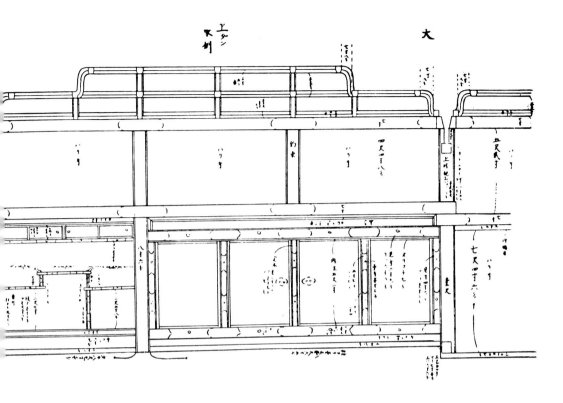

tors with striking murals in brilliant colors. For example, the *ohiroma* in the Ninomaru Compound in the Nijo Castle complex has *fusuma* on which there is a gigantic pine painted in glowing colors on a gold ground. Since opulent designs were not necessary in private quarters, the use of such murals was limited to the entrance hall and the audience quarters. The *shiroshoin* of the Nijo Castle Ninomaru Compound, which was the shogun's *gozanoma,* or private residential suite, has quiet paintings in black and white on its *fusuma.*

If you visit the Nijo Castle grounds now, you will be impressed by the overall appearance of the grand *shoin* structures under their massive tiled roofs (Fig. 100). The enormous gables are decorated with shiny gold fittings, and the brilliance of the openwork frieze under the eaves of the *karahafu-*gabled roof of the *kurumayose* (Figs. 101, 117) is particularly outstanding. The *ohiroma* and *kuroshoin*

(Fig. 123), which together cast a patterned shadow on the pond, are one of the most beautiful spectacles of the *shoin* complex.

You may wonder who was allowed to enjoy this view of the castle in all its impressive splendor. Since the palanquins and carts of the aristocrats arrived at the *kurumayose* (Fig. 116), they saw the buildings only through the thin blinds of their vehicles; these visitors, then, perceived the grandeur of the castle through the opulence of its interior. The splendid exteriors were intended as ostentatious display for the lower aristocrats and daimyos, who had to leave their carts and palanquins outside the gate and enter the castle grounds on foot, and as a showcase of authority for retainers and commoners.

To heighten the display, the large gables of the *tozamurai* (the quarters near the gate, usually adjoining the *genkan,* serving as a waiting room) and

*107. Tokonoma and* chigaidana *in* gakumonjo, *originally the study hall, of Kyoto Imperial Palace. 1855. Kyoto.*

the *ohiroma* were constructed to face the main entrance gate on the south of the compound so that the number of buildings in the compound appeared doubled to those passing through the gate into the yard in front of the *kurumayose.* Since the yard was at the entrance to the palace complex, a view of the buildings was presented to all visitors. During this period, however, it was not anticipated that anyone would walk about the garden to look at the buildings from different angles as we do today. The daimyos' suburban villas with large gardens and the detached palaces like Katsura in Kyoto were exceptions in that they were meant to be part of the gardens in which they were built.

A large roof that could be seen from afar was one means of impressing commoners, who were not allowed inside the grounds, with the splendor of the palace. Of the buildings located in the innermost part of daimyos' residences in Edo, only the kitchen had a decorated gable, since it had the tallest rooftop. The roofs of the other buildings were not visible from outside the compound and were thus reduced in height and had simple decorations. Reduction in the height of the roofs of buildings also occurred in the Hommaru Compound of Edo Castle.

When the foundation of the Tokugawa government became solidified so that its authority and prestige were sufficiently conveyed by the outer structures of Edo Castle, the tall, sweeping roof of the *ohiroma* building became low. The buildings in the Hommaru Compound were frequently repaired and expanded, and by the 1640s they were almost invisible from the outside. By the middle of the Edo period, exterior appearances were totally ignored not only in Edo Castle but in daimyo residences, as well: the gardens were surrounded by fences and hedges and only the interiors of buildings were elaborately decorated.

*108. Tokonoma and* chigaidana *in* hojo *of Honen-in. C. 1680. Kyoto.*

NEW TRENDS   Among elements found in *shoin*-style rooms used for official functions, only the *chigaidana* underwent substantial changes in style. The structures built under direct Tokugawa supervision, such as Kyoto Imperial Palace, were each often the responsibility of one construction commissioner or carpentry supervisor. The residents, including the emperor, the retired emperor, the retired empress, and the princesses, had little to say about design. When on rare occasions their suggestions were followed, they were recorded in the relevant documents as changes made in deference to the imperial wishes. Otherwise, the buildings were constructed and the rooms were decorated according to tradition.

The daimyos, however, often had considerable independence because their administrative units were much smaller than the central government's. They were not burdened by hereditary rules and customs as was the central government, and in their architecture the daimyos felt relatively free to change designs and plans.

Within the central government, even changes effected by the shogun or by any of his advisers were extremely rare. The layouts and plans of the principal buildings in Edo Castle were customarily handed down from generation to generation under the care of high-ranking officials. During the two hundred and sixty-five years after August 1, 1603, when Ieyasu returned to Edo Castle's Hommaru Palace as the shogun, the palace was either renovated or completely rebuilt five times—in 1637, 1640, 1659, 1845, and 1860—but its principal buildings did not undergo any major changes after the building complex was completed in 1640.

It is not known who in the hierarchy of carpenters made decisions on the details of design. But since the various rules and precedents of the Toku-

*109. Tokonoma and* chigaidana *of* jodan *in* shinden *of Emman-in; note additional tatami in* jodan. *1619; moved to present site 1647. Otsu, Shiga Prefecture. (See also Figure 86.)*

gawa government were established between the 1620s and 1640s, it would seem likely that the decorations used in the *shiroshoin* and *kuroshoin* in the Hommaru Compound of Osaka Castle would have been adopted in the *shiroshoin* and *kuroshoin* of Edo Castle. However, this was not the case. The measurements of the pillars, *tenjo nageshi, uchinori nageshi,* and doorsills of Osaka Castle are similar to those of Nijo Castle, not to those of Edo Castle. The *chigaidana* in Osaka and Nijo castles are so similar, in fact, that it is reasonable to assume they were chosen by the same person. The combinations of the two *chigaidana* sections laid out in an L-shape in the corner and the arrangement of the staggered shelves are the same both in the *kuroshoin* of Nijo Castle (Figs. 81, 122) and in the *ohiroma* in the Hommaru Compound of Osaka Castle (Fig. 106). It is possible that among the superintendents and carpentry supervisors involved in the construction of the two com-

plexes, either Kobori Enshu or Nakai Masatomo, or perhaps both in cooperation, supervised the interior decorating.

Even with all the renovation and reconstruction there had been only one change in Edo Castle, an alteration in the front area of the Hommaru Compound. During the Kyoho era (1716–36), Arai Hakuseki (1656–1725), a Confucian scholar brought into the administration as a shogunal councilor, argued that the placement of a gate inside the compound between the front gate and the main building, the *ohiroma,* wrongly indicated the shogun's status as being inferior to that of the chief adviser to the emperor and to that of the great minister. He recommended that the shogun erect and use instead a roofed gate with two main pillars and four supporting pillars. The recommendation was accepted and the gate was built. But after several years the former gate was again put to use because

*110.* Jodan *and* chodaigamae *in* tsune no goten *of Kyoto Imperial Palace; note formal arrangement of additional tatami in* jodan. *1855. Kyoto.*

the new gate was unsuited to the traditional custom of having soldiers pass through the gate with banners held aloft. Because the times were peaceful, arguments based on martial precedent did not make much sense; but precedent, once set, worked to preserve tradition. All government bureaucrats, from those of the highest rank down through the lower echelons, lived in the safety of officialdom; and to suggest reform except in dire necessity often meant placing oneself in jeopardy or losing a promotion.

Whether in Edo Castle, the Imperial Palace, local castles, or in other buildings in which large organizations were quartered, the personal tastes of the principal resident could effect only minor changes in plan and design. Comparison of the plans of the buildings and the uses of the rooms in the Hommaru Compound in Edo Castle with those of the daimyos' residences shows clearly that where

there was less shackling by tradition structures were adapted to new uses and functions. Thus the single-row arrangement of two or three reception rooms in the *shoin* style was adopted by the daimyos; and this plan, which eventually became the basic arrangement for the modern residential house, was not limited to the residences of the warrior class.

To be sure, the style was most commonly adopted by the warriors; but during that period, life styles were more or less similar among all those of the upper strata, which included aristocrats and priests, as well as warriors. Accordingly, all groups adopted similar architectural designs in their residences. However, the Imperial Palace and the residences of the highest-ranking nobility—such as the families who provided the chief advisers to the emperor and therefore performed traditional rituals as part of their function—maintained the traditional *shuden* style, that is, with a *chumon* and *kurumayose*.

The Tokugawa government classified people according to occupation and set strict regulations against changing the classifications. Of the four major classes—warrior, farmer, artisan, and merchant—the latter three, being categorized as commoners, were forbidden to construct a *shoin.* The restrictions were very detailed: for example, building a *shoin* with a tokonoma, *chigaidana, uchinori nageshi* and *tenjo nageshi,* and a *tsukeshoin,* and displaying a mural in brilliant colors on a gold ground, were all forbidden to the commoners. Village heads were the only commoners who were officially permitted to have a *shoin,* since they had to host daimyos and other officials. Most farmers and townspeople had to wait until the Meiji Restoration before they could use a tokonoma and other room decorations in their houses.

In the face of such restrictions, some of the rich merchants and farmers were disobedient, either secretly or in open defiance, and the number of these people increased as time passed. Over the years many of the warriors, from the most powerful Tokugawa family down to the lowest-ranking foot soldiers, exhausted their financial resources and borrowed heavily from rich commoners. Consequently, the warrior class lost much of its authority and could seldom enforce its restrictive regulations. By the latter part of the Edo period, some of the residences of the wealthy merchants exceeded those of the upper classes in size, as well as in the money lavished upon them. The homes of these wealthy commoners were, however, basically copies of the upper-class residences and were not unique creations.

The *shoin* style was also used in the residential structures in temple complexes. This was particularly true of the major temples, whose chief priests came from the imperial and other important aristocratic families. Among the *shoin* and residential structures built during the Edo period that survive to this day, many are found in temple grounds, far from the busy sections of town, where they have been less exposed to the perils of destruction.

# CHAPTER FOUR

# The Tokugawa Shoin

NIJO CASTLE Nijo Castle (Fig. 111) in Kyoto was completed in 1603 as the fortified residence of Tokugawa Ieyasu, the victorious general who had only recently become the most powerful man in Japan. This castle was built when the emperor's proxy conferred on him the title *Seii-tai-shogun* (Barbarian-Quelling Generalissimo). This ceremony was of great importance to Ieyasu, for although he was indeed the de facto ruler, he needed to legitimize his and his descendants' right to wield the power he had taken with his sword. The emperor did not hold actual power, but authority from the imperial throne was necessary for maintaining continued unity of the nation. Ieyasu's predecessors, the generals Oda Nobunaga and Toyotomi Hideyoshi, who had also ruled the country, had not received this title. With the deaths of these men, their families' fortunes went into sharp decline; and the lesson was not lost on Ieyasu, who was determined to found a lasting and stable dynasty.

Although Nijo Castle was constructed as a residence for Ieyasu, he had his headquarters in Fushimi Castle, south of Kyoto; and even after becoming shogun he continued to administer the affairs of state from there. A later shogun moved the administrative headquarters to Edo; subsequently, Nijo Castle was used only to accommodate the Tokugawa shoguns when they were in Kyoto to be received at the Imperial Palace. It became little more than a stopping place where the shogun changed to a more appropriate costume before going on to the Imperial Palace, for it was but rarely that an emperor granted an audience outside the Imperial Palace.

The first imperial visit to a warrior's residence is said to have taken place in 1408, when Emperor Gokomatsu (1377–1433) visited the Ashikaga shogun Yoshimitsu (1358–1408) in Kyoto. Later, Emperor Gohanazono (1419–70) visited the Ashikaga shogun Yoshinori (1393–1441) at his residence in Kyoto. Oda Nobunaga, the sixteenth-century warlord who almost fulfilled his dream of reunifying the country, had had a room in Azuchi Castle prepared for an imperial visit. Apparently he had intended to welcome the reigning emperor after pacifying all Japan. In April, 1588, the military dictator Toyotomi Hideyoshi had the honor of welcoming Emperor Goyozei (1571–1617) at the Juraku-dai castle-palace in the Fushimi Castle grounds.

The Tokugawa shoguns, having gained military hegemony with Ieyasu's victory at Sekigahara in 1600, quite naturally wanted to follow their predecessors and welcome an emperor to Nijo Castle, their official mansion. When it was decided that the third Tokugawa shogun, Iemitsu (1604–51), would receive Emperor Gomizuno-o (1596–1680) at Nijo Castle, it was necessary to expand the castle to make it a fitting place to receive an imperial visit. A new Hommaru Compound was built; the old Hommaru Compound then became the

*111. Nijo Castle as shown in screens depicting the Kyoto area. Seventeenth century. Shoko-ji temple, Kyoto.*

Ninomaru Compound. The palace in the Nino-maru Compound was completely renovated to accommodate Iemitsu; and a new palace—the Gyoko Goten—was specially built as a temporary residence for the emperor.

This vast architectural project was supervised by six magistrates: Kobori Masakazu, who is better known to us as Kobori Enshu and was then the chief magistrate in Fushimi, Kyoto; Gomi Kin'e-mon Toyonao; Ono Sozaemon Sadanori; Sunami Shume Shigekatsu; Nakanobo Sakon Chobei; and Ichikawa Shigezaemon Mitsutomo. The actual construction was directed by Nakai Masatomo, the head carpentry supervisor in Kyoto for the Toku-gawa government. Sharing equal rank and respon-sibility with Nakai Masatomo, by far the most important of the six magistrates was Kobori Enshu.

In 1611 and 1619 Enshu had worked on the con-struction of the Imperial Palace, and he was wide-ly recognized as the best magistrate of the time. Enshu was also distinguished in painting, poetry, flower arrangement, pottery making, and architec-ture; and he founded a school of tea ceremony and designed numerous gardens, many of which are extant today. With such impressive abilities, Ko-bori Enshu was perfectly suited for his role in the work of expanding Nijo Castle. He not only super-vised the construction and decoration of the Gyoko Goten but also took charge of the construction of the principle buildings in the Hommaru Com-pound—the *ohiroma,* the *shoin,* and the *gozanoma* (the master's residential suite)—as well as the two *gozanoma* buildings in the Ninomaru Compound that were to accommodate the shogun.

112. *Aerial view of Nijo Castle: upper left, Hommaru Compound, with donjon foundation visible at extreme left; lower right, Ninomaru Compound; extreme lower right, eastern main gate to the castle. Kyoto.*

Even if we were to judge solely on the basis of the participation of such an illustrious man as Kobori Enshu, we could see the great importance that the Tokugawas attached to an imperial visit. However, we have the official Tokugawa record, *An Account of the Imperial Visit,* as further support. The following passage clearly indicates the tremendous Tokugawa resolve to outdo any previous imperial visit: "At this time the benevolent rule of the government of imperial court and shogunate had spread far into the nine countries of pagans and the eight countries of barbarians. It was most commendable that the government should have studied ancient things, revived obsolete customs, and had the honor of winning an imperial visit. The Kitayama structure [the site of an earlier imperial visit] cannot be said to have been as good as it should have been,

and the splendid Juraku-dai [where Hideyoshi received Emperor Goyozei] left much to be desired; but who in the future will not admire Nijo Castle, where the ceremony was held?"

Preparations for construction were begun in 1624, two years before the imperial visit. It seems that before expansion of the castle, the Ninomaru Compound contained five buildings, all connected by interior passageways, or covered corridors. Moreover, it appears that the carpenters simply followed the pattern of the old Ninomaru Palace in building the new one. When the Gyoko Goten was added to the southwest corner of the compound, it was connected to the buildings in both the Ninomaru and Hommaru compounds by corridors. The complexity and extent of these corridors are shown clearly in the foldout facing page 128.

*114. The South Gate of Nijo ▷ Castle. Kyoto.*

In front of the Gyoko Goten was a large yard covered with white sand. The Gyoko Goten itself was an impressive structure, measuring thirteen bays from east to west and eleven bays from north to south (a bay is the distance between two structural columns; the actual measured distance varied from era to era). In conformity with architectural conventions of the time, it was made completely of the highly valued Japanese cypress: even the shingles were of cypress bark. The interior of the Gyoko Goten was partitioned with *fusuma* into eleven rooms of various sizes. The three rooms on the west side of the Gyoko Goten were called, from north to south, the north, middle, and south *jodan*. The floors of these *jodan* rooms were raised one step above the adjoining *gedan,* or standard-level rooms.

While the important south *jodan* and its adjoining *gedan* to the east were used for formal functions, the north *jodan,* which faced a garden and pond, was of a more informal nature. Its walls and *fusuma*

were covered with a mural depicting exotic Tartars, and it was here that ceremonial drinking was done. During the ceremonies—when three cups of sakè were exchanged three times—the emperor and the shogun sat facing each other, the emperor on the north side of the room and the shogun on the south.

Unlike the north and south *jodan,* which were both used for holding audiences, the middle *jodan* was a living room. In it were a black lacquered shelf for the emperor's personal belongings, a dressing table with an inlaid design, and a pitcher of water. On the east side of the room the ornate *chodaigamae* opened onto the *chodai,* or bedroom. In the *chodai* were an imperial sword, a bed made of tatami mats, a clothes stand, a clothes chest, an armrest, and a box containing tooth-dyeing utensils and other dressing items. All these splendidly lacquered objects with their inlaid gold and silver designs, together with various dinner sets, had been prepared for this special occasion by Kobori Enshu.

*115. The* karahafu-*gabled gate to the Ninomaru Compound of Nijo Castle. 1626. Kyoto.*

Just before noon on the sixth of September, 1626, the rain that had been falling on Kyoto since the previous night stopped. Emperor Gomizuno-o was seated on a cushion in the large, twenty-four-mat south *jodan* of the Gyoko Goten. Seated near him was his brother-in-law Iemitsu, the third of the Tokugawa shoguns. The emperor's father-in-law, the retired shogun, Hidetada (1579–1632), was also seated nearby. The three men were drinking together. The tokonoma alcove and the *chigaidana* behind the emperor emphasized his place of honor. The *chigaidana* were decorated with a lacquered bookrest, an inkstone, and gold and silver incense utensils.

A painting by Kano Tan'yu (1602–74), a nephew of Eitoku and the best painter of the period, covered the walls and *fusuma* of both the south *jodan* and its adjoining *gedan*, where retainers and lesser-ranking guests—ineligible to be seated in the *jodan*—were

admitted. Most appropriately for an imperial seat, Tan'yu's painting, in brilliant colors on a gold ground, depicted a virtuous Chinese emperor. This work had been carefully chosen for the two rooms because the emperor would be granting audiences there and they would be the imperial seat when court dances and the martial arts were performed in the south yard.

On the ninth of September, four days after the emperor's arrival, Iemitsu arranged a staging of Noh plays and invited the emperor to the *ohiroma* of the Ninomaru Palace (Fig. 118). Possibly he wanted to show off his own quarters, which he could do to advantage, since the Noh stage was immediately south of the *ohiroma*. The *ohiroma*, the formal reception hall or audience suite, was the most important room in the warrior's residence. It is not surprising, then, that in the Ninomaru Compound the *ohiroma* was the most important and most lavishly decor-

116. Kurumayose, *foreground, and* tozamurai *in Ninomaru Compound of Nijo Castle. 1626. Kyoto. (See also Figure 101.)*

117. *Detail of openwork frieze beneath eaves of* kurumayose *in the Ninomaru Compound of Nijo Castle. 1626. Kyoto. (See also Figure 101.)*

118. Southern view of kuroshoin, left, and ohiroma, right, in Ninomaru Compound of Nijo Castle. 1626. Kyoto. (See also Figure 123.)

120. Reenactment of an audience in ohiroma in Ninomaru Compound of Nijo Castle, Kyoto. (See also Figure 99.)

ated building. Although the *ohiroma* in the Ninomaru Palace was renovated prior to the emperor's visit to make it more suitable as a shogunal mansion, the work done on it was less elaborate than that done on the Gyoko Goten, perhaps in deference to the emperor. Altogether the carpenters employed for the Gyoko Goten labored for a total of 39,179 man-days, and for the *ohiroma*, only 20,250, although the *ohiroma* was a much larger structure.

Nevertheless, the *ohiroma* to which the shogun invited the emperor appropriately expressed the status of the shogun, the actual ruler of the country. The *ohiroma* as seen today was indeed fit for the supreme military leader: the forty-eight-mat *jodan* (Figs. 99, 120) has a coffered coved ceiling (Fig. 121); and the tokonoma, which is almost six meters wide, is flanked on the west by a *tsukeshoin* about one-

third of a meter above the floor and on the east by both *chigaidana* and *chodaigamae*. A giant pine is painted on the wall of the tokonoma, and on the walls and *fusuma* surrounding the room is a painting of an old pine by Tan'yu and the artists of his school. The two rooms comprising the audience suite, the *jodan* and the *gedan*, are only separated by a difference in the elevation of their floors and by a *kokabe* and *otoshigake*, which can be seen quite clearly in Figure 99. As illustrated in Figure 120, when granting audiences, the shogun sat in the center of the *jodan*, with his back to the tokonoma and the *chigaidana*, facing his subjects, who sat far from him, in the *gedan*.

The floor plans of the Gyoko Goten prepared for Emperor Gomizuno-o's visit and of the *ohiroma* in the Ninomaru Compound are similar, although

◁ 119. Garden in Ninomaru Compound of Nijo Castle. 1626. Kyoto. (See also Figure 123.)

121. *Double-coved, coffered, and latticed ceiling of* jodan *in* ohiroma *in Ninomaru Compound of Nijo Castle. 1626. Kyoto. (See also Figure 99.)*

the rooms of each were used differently. For example, because the *ohiroma* was frequently used by the shogun for holding audiences, the *jodan* was provided with all the warrior-class traditional decorative elements, such as a tokonoma, *chigaidana, chodaigamae,* a *tsukeshoin,* and even an ornate coffered coved ceiling. However, because the Gyoko Goten was built for the emperor and imperial residences were very simply decorated, its *jodan* were not so elaborate. Only the south *jodan* was decorated to any great extent, and it had only a tokonoma and *chigaidana.*

We note another difference in the function of the *chodai* in these two structures. In the *ohiroma* the *chodai,* just east of the *jodan,* was not used as a bedroom: the shogun's bedroom was in the *shiroshoin* which was in fact his *gozanoma,* or private residential suite. When he gave an audience he left the *gozanoma* and entered the *ohiroma chodai,* which was

simply used as a waiting room. He entered the *jodan* from this room only after the daimyos who were to be received had prostrated themselves in the *gedan;* and he went directly back into the *chodai* after the audience. Along with this change in the function of the *chodai,* the *chodaigamae* lost their original purpose and became merely grand doors studded with metalwork embossed with golden hollyhocks (the Tokugawa crest), and with glossy, black-lacquered sills and lintels—grand doors through which the shogun made his entrance.

However, in the Gyoko Goten the *chodai,* located next to the middle *jodan,* was actually used as a bedroom by the emperor because no separate residential quarters had been prepared for him. Thus the striking *chodaigamae* in the Gyoko Goten, which were covered with purple brocade and had very colorful tassels woven in five colors, retained their original function. It should be pointed out that it

122. Tsukeshoin, *tokonoma*, *L-shaped* chigaidana, *and* chodaigamae *in* jodan *of* kuroshoin *in Ninomaru Compound of Nijo Castle. 1626. Kyoto. (See also Figure 81.)*

123. Kuroshoin, *left, and* ohiroma, *right, viewed across garden pond in Ninomaru Compound of Nijo Castle. 1626. Kyoto. (See also Figure 118.)*

was through neither an oversight nor an intended slight on the part of the Tokugawas that only the Gyoko Goten was constructed for the emperor: long tradition dictated that only one structure be erected as a temporary palace for an imperial visit.

OSAKA CASTLE   The Hommaru Palace (Fig. 124) in the Hommaru Compound of the Osaka Castle complex was rebuilt by the Tokugawa government at about the same time as the various buildings in the Nijo Castle complex. Since the Hommaru Palace was used as the formal Tokugawa mansion in Kinki (the Kyoto, Osaka, and Nara area) after Fushimi Castle, the old shogunal headquarters, was demolished, a resident administrator was always stationed here until the

end of Tokugawa rule. It was used to accommodate the last Tokugawa shogun, Keiki (1837–1913), during his visit to Kyoto to surrender to the revolutionaries of the Meiji Restoration, the political revolution that resulted in the abolition of the Tokugawa military government in 1868.

Until recently, we knew only the number of laborers employed for, the sizes of, and the rough plans for the buildings in the Hommaru Compound of the Osaka Castle complex because the Hommaru Palace did not survive past the Meiji Restoration. Very little information is contained in the drawings and documents (Figs. 37, 124) owned by the descendants of the Nakai family, who served as the shogunal head carpentry supervisor in Kyoto. A few years ago, however, I had an unexpected op-

124. *Composite plan of Hommaru Palace of Osaka Castle, according to specifications in documents belonging to Nakai and Furuhashi families. (See also Figure 37.)* ▷

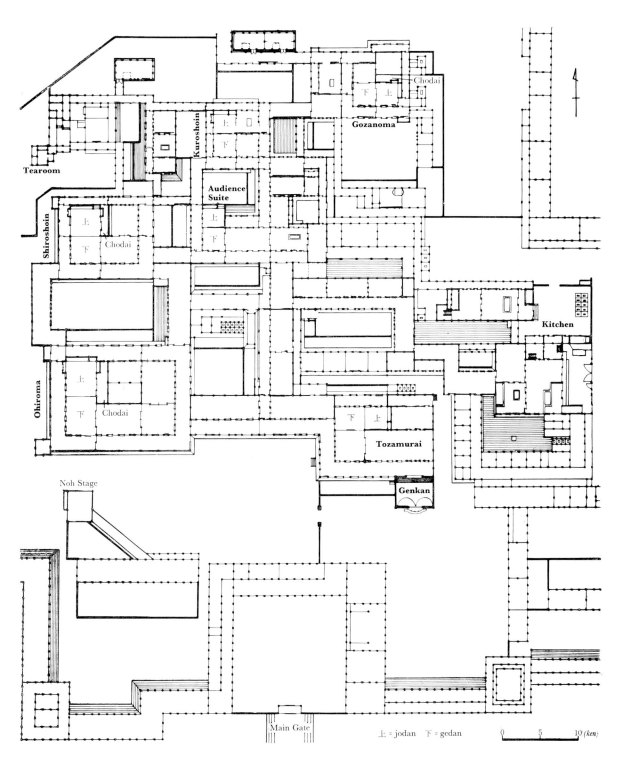

Tearoom

Kuroshoin

上
下

Gozanoma

Chodai

上
下

Audience
Suite

上
下

Shiroshoin

上
下 Chodai

Kitchen

Ohiroma

上
下 Chodai

Tozamurai

下 上

Genkan

Noh Stage

Main Gate

上 = jodan    下 = gedan

0    5    10 (ken)

125. Jodan *of front* shoin *in Hommaru Compound of Nagoya Castle in Aichi Prefecture; note* fusuma *and* latticelike ramma *separating* jodan *and* gedan. *Completed, 1615; destroyed by bombing, 1945.*

portunity to see some drawings of the Hommaru Palace (Fig. 106) among documents handed down in the Furuhashi family, whose ancestors were under the supervision of the Nakai family. The Furuhashis, among the head carpenters in Osaka, were placed in charge of the quarters for the ladies-in-waiting and other structures of the Imperial Palace during the late 1850s. Since the family was of good lineage, its members most likely had opportunities to enter the Osaka Castle grounds.

The Furuhashi documents are not very old; they were drawn more than two centuries after the two-and-a-half-year period, 1626 to 1629, when the palace was under construction; and the drawings include no description of the exteriors except for a cross section illustrating a small part of the outer-most zone. But the interiors are shown in great detail as interior development drawings with actual measurements indicated. According to other records, extensive repair work was begun on the Hommaru Palace of Osaka Castle in November, 1845; and it was restored to its original appearance in June, 1847, so the Furuhashi drawings most probably date from this period. The documents also include two sets of memoranda and illustrations dated 1868.

The buildings of the Nijo and Osaka castle complexes share many common features. Records of the repair work begun in 1954 on the Ninomaru Palace of Nijo Castle reveal that some of the beams of the *ohiroma* had been marked as materials intended for Osaka Castle. It is not known when the

126. *Sumi-no-e room of Rinshun-kaku, with* tokonoma, chigaidana, *and greatly simplified* tsukeshoin. *1649; moved to present site* ▷
*1915. Sankei-en, Yokohama. (See also Figures 157, 158.)*

*127 (overleaf). Tokonoma and tsukeshoin in main room of* kuroshoin *of Nishi Hongan-ji* ▷
*temple, viewed from second room. 1657. Kyoto. (See also Figure 154.)*

129. *Tokonoma*, *tsukeshoin*, *and small* jodan *in main room of small* shoin *of Manshu-in; the imperial crest (the chrysanthemum) is used decoratively in the* ramma. *1655. Kyoto. (See also Figure 128.)*

◁ 128. *Large* shoin *and, just visible in right background, small* shoin *of Manshu-in. 1656. Kyoto. (See also Figure 129.)*

132. *View of garden from shoin of Jiko-in. C. 1664. Yamato-Koriyama, Nara Prefecture.*

*133. Tokonoma and* chigaidana *in* kuroshoin *in Hommaru Compound of Nagoya Castle in Aichi Prefecture. Completed 1615; destroyed by bombing 1945.*

construction of the Hommaru Palace of Osaka Castle was actually planned, although the temporary palace was completed in 1624. The exact planning dates for the expansion of Nijo Castle, the construction of its Hommaru Compound, the Ninomaru Compound, and the Gyoko Goten are also unknown. But if the materials originally intended for Osaka Castle were used in Nijo Castle, the expansion of Nijo Castle cannot have been done very much before 1624.

With regard to the construction of Osaka Castle, we know that Kobori Enshu was the superintendent of works and that the head carpentry supervisor for the palace in the Hommaru Compound was Nakai Masatomo. Other superintendents of works were: Kitami, Nakamura Magobei, Nakanobo Sakon Chobei, Yamada Gorobei, Mamiya San'emon, Negoro Ukyo, and Sunami Shume Shigekatsu. Some of these commissioners served in the same

capacities with Enshu and Masatomo for the expansion of Nijo Castle. Kobori Enshu, after completing work on the temporary palace in the Osaka Castle complex, took charge of the expansion of Nijo Castle and then returned to work on Osaka Castle. In Kyoto there was no official organization of carpenters other than that under Nakai Masatomo, so it is generally believed that Osaka and Nijo castles were built by the same group of craftsmen.

The major buildings of the Hommaru Palace in the Osaka Castle complex were the *tozamurai*, the *ohiroma*, the *kohiroma* (the minor reception hall, which is the *shiroshoin* in this complex), the *kuroshoin*, the *gozanoma*, the residential suite, and the kitchen. Other important quarters were separate chambers for councilors, servants, the superintendent of documents, and other individuals. The Nakai drawing in Figure 124, which depicts an

*134. Tokonoma,* chigaidana, *and* chodaigamae *in Joraku-den in Hommaru Compound of Nagoya Castle in Aichi Prefecture. Completed 1634; destroyed by bombing 1945.*

earlier plan, also shows a tearoom and a room connected with tea ceremony that were omitted in the drawings dating from the late Edo period. Structurally the Osaka Palace complex, based on the plans used for Edo Castle, resembles more closely the Hommaru Compound of Edo Castle than the Hommaru and Ninomaru compounds of Nijo Castle. In particular, the *shiroshoin* and *kuroshoin* of Osaka Castle include two adjacent rooms used exactly the same way as in Edo Castle. However, in terms of interior design Osaka Castle and Nijo Castle show many similarities.

Figure 135 gives measurements of the various interior structures in the principal buildings of the Hommaru Compound of Osaka Castle, the Ninomaru Compound of Nijo Castle, and the Hommaru Compound of Edo Castle, including the dimensions of the pillars, the depths of the lintels and the doorsills, the distance from the floor to the *uchinori*

*nageshi* (the decorative band or half-beam at the bottom of the *kokabe*), the width of the *sai* (the upper groove that supports the *fusuma,* whose tracks were made by nailing together several long, thin wooden strips rather than by cutting directly into the wooden beam, as was done for the tracks in the doorsill), the height of the *kokabe,* the height of the *arikabe* (literally, "ant wall," because of its small size; the small section of wall between the beam closest to the ceiling and the ceiling itself), and the depths of the *uchinori nageshi* and the *tenjo nageshi* (the band or half-beam at the top of the *kokabe*). Although these elements may be difficult to visualize, they are shown clearly in Figures 92 and 94.

From Figure 135, one can immediately see that the lintels and doorsills are of the same thickness in all the buildings in the Edo Castle compound; but in Nijo and Osaka castles their thickness varies with the thickness of the pillars. Also, while the

| Element | Edo Castle Hommaru Compound 1860 | | | | Osaka Castle Hommaru Compound 1629 | | | | | Nijo Castle Ninomaru Compound 1626 | | |
|---|---|---|---|---|---|---|---|---|---|---|---|---|
| | Ohiroma | Shiro-shoin | Kuro-shoin | Goza-noma | Ohiroma | Shiro-shoin | Kuro-shoin | Goza-noma | Audience suite | Ohiroma | Kuro-shoin | Shiro-shoin |
| Pillar thickness | 7.8 | 6.5 | 6.0 | 5.6 | 8.6 | 7.2 | 6.2 | 6.6 | 6.5 | 8.0 | 7.0 | 6.5 |
| Lintel depth | 2.0 | 2.0 | 2.0 | 2.0 | 2.5 | 2.2 | 2.0 | 2.4 | 2.0 | 2.3 | 2.2 | 2.0 |
| Doorsill depth | 2.0 | 2.0 | 2.0 | 2.0 | 2.8 | 2.5 | 2.4 | 2.4 | 2.3 | 2.5 | 2.6 | 2.5 |
| *Sai* width | 0.8 | 0.9 | — | — | 1.2 | 1.2 | 1.4 | 1.2 | 1.2 | 1.1 | 1.1 | 1.1 |
| Floor to *uchinori nageshi* | 72.5 | 61.2 | 61.1 | 60.0 | 73.5 | 72.8 | 64.5 | 64.3 | 64.3 | 71.5 | 71.2 | 65.2 |
| *Kokabe* height | 58.0 | 50.0 | 45.0 | 51.0 | 51.8 | 43.7 | 51.0 | 64.8 | 46.0 | 48.5 | 45.0 | 38.4 |
| *Arikabe* height | 8.0 | 5.8 | 6.0 | 6.0 | — | 7.0 | 5.6 | 6.7 | 5.9 | 8.4 | 7.2 | 5.7 |
| *Uchinori nageshi* depth | 7.0 | 5.8 | 5.4 | 5.0 | 7.0 | 6.0 | 5.0 | 5.5 | 5.4 | 6.7 | 6.0 | 5.2 |
| *Tenjo nageshi* depth | — | 5.2 | 4.2 | 4.0 | 7.0 | 6.0 | 5.0 | 5.5 | 5.3 | 6.7 | 6.0 | 5.2 |

135. *Measurements of the principal structures in the Hommaru compounds of Edo and Osaka castles and in the Ninomaru Compound of Nijo Castle. All measurements are given in* sun, *about 1.19 inches.*

*uchinori nageshi* and *tenjo nageshi* in Nijo and Osaka castles are of the same depth, this is not true in Edo Castle. This table shows that the interiors of Nijo and Osaka castles were very similar, in contrast to the interior of Edo Castle. This may well be because Nijo and Osaka castles were built in the mid-1620s, whereas Edo Castle was built in the mid-nineteenth century.

EDO CASTLE  During the administration of the second shogun, Hidetada, the Tokugawa government moved its headquarters to Edo Castle. Subsequently, in 1619, Fushimi Castle in Kyoto, from which the first shogun, Ieyasu, had administered the affairs of state, was demolished. The Hommaru Palace built by Ieyasu in the Hommaru Compound of Edo Castle was gradually altered to make it a more fitting seat for a shogun to rule from. Site plans of the Hommaru Compound

in its entirety as constructed in 1640 are owned by Yoshihide Okuma, an architect well known in Japan today. There are also plans of the *ohiroma* in the Hommaru Palace drawn during the Hoei era (1701–11) by Kora Konen, the Tokugawas' head carpentry supervisor in Edo; and site plans include the structures as rebuilt in 1659. The plans owned by Okuma and a later set, drawn in 1718, show all the main structures, including the *tozamurai* (the quarters near the gate that functioned as a waiting room), the *ohiroma*, the *shiroshoin* and *kuroshoin* (used as minor reception halls), and the *gozanoma*.

The 1640 plans, titled *Notes and Elevations of the Ohiroma: Plans of the Ohiroma in the Hommaru Compound as Constructed in the Seventeenth Year of the Kan'ei Era*, record: "This is the *ohiroma* rebuilt after the palace in the Hommaru Compound first burned down. This palace burned on January 19, 1657;

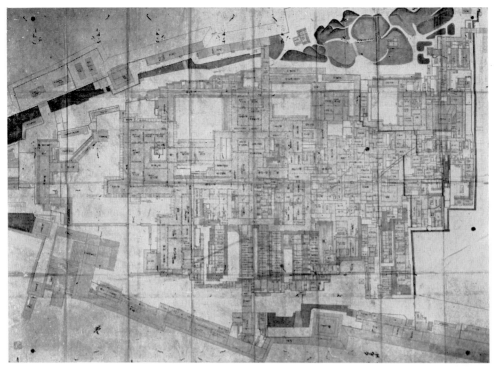

*136. Kora's ground plan of Edo Castle (the most accurate extant plan). 1718. Hibiya Library.*

the present palace was constructed with its surrounding structures in 1659." A comparison of the *ohiroma* shown in this document with the *ohiroma* shown in later Kora plans (Fig. 136) reveals many minor differences. It is difficult to decide which of the two documents gives a more accurate description of the *ohiroma;* but in both instances, the *ohiroma* has a tokonoma, *chigaidana,* a *tsukeshoin,* and *chodaigamae* in the main room of the building. In addition, the *ohiroma* contains a suite with a *jodan, chudan,* and *gedan;* there is also a *chumon,* a short inner corridor, projecting from the southeast corner of the building.

*Notes and Elevations* also records that the *ohiroma* shown in the plans deviates from the conventional *ohiroma* and makes reference to the fact that the *ohiroma* in the residence of the head of the military government at Kamakura, which held power from 1185 to 1336, measured six bays by seven bays and

had a *chumon,* a *kurumayose* with a *karahafu* gable, a wooden-floored tokonoma, and a *chodai.* It further records that the *ohiroma* constructed during and following the Ashikaga shogunate (1336–1568) had a *chumon* and a *kurumayose* with a *karahafu* gable.

Similar information concerning *ohiroma* appears in *Sanko Ochibo Shu* (a 1746 collection of accounts of events in Edo) and in the *Ryuei Hikan* (an early eighteenth-century collection of rites, rules, manners, and precedents of the Tokugawa government). Adding a *chumon* and a *kurumayose* with a *karahafu* gable when building the *ohiroma* came to be known as the *shuden* style. From these plans and documents we know that the Tokugawas, as the leaders of the samurai class, tried to maintain the traditional style of architecture used in the mansion of the head of the military government in Kamakura.

The appearance of the Hommaru Compound of Edo Castle prior to 1640 cannot be ascertained in

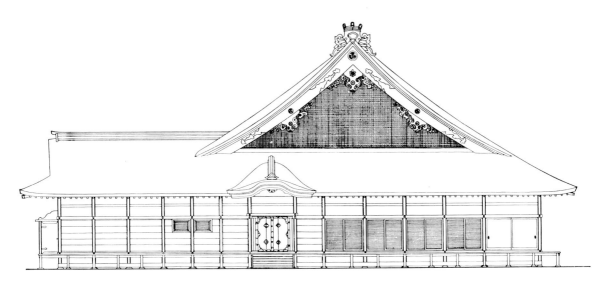

*137. Elevation of the* ohiroma *in Hommaru Compound of Edo Castle, according to specifications in documents in the collection of* Yoshihide Okuma *dated 1640.*

the absence of the original plans, but the main components—the *ohiroma,* the *shiroshoin,* the *kuroshoin,* and the *gozanoma*—were also built in Osaka Castle, which was extensively renovated in 1624 to replace Fushimi Castle. Various written records, one dated 1615, indicate that the same structures were built in the Hommaru compounds of both castles. Thus one may conclude that the Hommaru Compound of Edo Castle dates from Ieyasu's time. There were also similarities in the basic structures and the use of decorative elements in the Ninomaru Palace of the Nijo Castle complex and in the Hommaru Palace of the Edo Castle complex. The only differences are that a *chumon* projects from the southeast corner of the *ohiroma* of Edo Castle and the *tozamurai* in Edo Castle is not as large as that in Nijo Castle (see foldout following page 128).

The *tozamurai* (literally, "distant samurai") had originally been built near the *ohiroma* of the war-

rior's residence as quarters for his guards. During peaceful times the original type of *tozamurai* was no longer needed, and a *tozamurai* with a *genkan* or a *shikidai* (the waiting room for retainers) came to serve as the formal entry into the residence in place of the *kurumayose* and *chumon.* This was especially true of the large-scale residences of ruling warriors built after 1657.

The Hommaru Palace of Nagoya Castle (built by the Nakai family for the Tokugawas) and the palace in the Hommaru Compound of Nijo Castle no longer had the *shuden*-style *chumon* and *kurumayose;* the *tozamurai* of the Ninomaru Palace of Nijo Castle is the last built on so massive a scale. The *tozamurai* built simultaneously in the Hommaru Compound is much smaller; the same is true of both the *tozamurai* in the Hommaru Compound of Osaka Castle and the *tozamurai* in the Hommaru Compound of Nagoya Castle. The *tozamurai* in the

*138. Shoin of Katsura Detached Palace. C. 1645. Kyoto.*

Ninomaru Compound of Nijo Castle retains the characteristics of the traditional *tozamurai,* as can be seen both in *Shomei* (the five-volume work on design techniques) and in *Drawings of the Kamakura Shogun's Mansion.* The latter depicts the residences belonging to warriors during the period between 1550 and 1615.

Although military hegemony had fallen into Ieyasu's hands, the people were still restless, and the vast scale of the old-style *tozamurai* in Nijo Castle was needed to accommodate the numerous retainers who accompanied Ieyasu on his visits to Kyoto. Later *tozamurai*, reflecting the peacefulness of the times following the Sieges of Osaka Castle, were geared to the entertainment of guests and developed into the modern *genkan,* or front entry hall.

Other than in the *ohiroma* of the Edo Castle Hommaru Palace, the Tokugawa government employed the *shuden* style, with a *chumon* and a *kurumayose*, in only one other structure during its rule—the audience suite (Fig. 73) of the Nyogo Gosho, or Empress's Palace, in the Imperial Palace complex in Kyoto. The Empress's Palace was built when Tokugawa Kazuko, one of Hidetada's daughters, joined the imperial household as the consort of Emperor Gomizuno-o. The Empress's Palace was built in 1619 on the site where the palace of the retired emperor Goyozei had been. The principal building of the Empress's Palace complex resembles the great audience hall of the Imperial Palace (Fig. 66). The main building (Fig. 88) was later moved to the Daikaku-ji temple in Sagano, Kyoto.

The audience suite of the Empress's Palace was in the *shuden* style and had a *chumon* and a *kuruma-yose* with a *karahafu*-gabled roof and a window of horizontal slats, a *jodan* under a coved-and-latticed ceiling, a wooden-floored tokonoma, *chigaidana,*

*139.* Jodan *in* hojo *of Konchi-in, with tokonoma and* tsukeshoin. *1624-44. Kyoto.*

*chodaigamae,* and a *tsukeshoin.* The audience suite was built as if to symbolize the participation of a member of the powerful Tokugawa family in the imperial household, and it remained in the Imperial Palace until Emperor Gomizuno-o retired. It was epoch-making to have a structure in the *shuden* style built in the Imperial Palace, and the building was an apparent attempt by the Tokugawas to pit this style symbolically against the aristocrats' traditional style of architecture, in which the *shinden,* used as the ceremonial quarters by the master of the house, had been the main building of the Empress's Palace.

After construction of the Empress's Palace, the *shuden* style was considered by the Tokugawa government as the most formal style of architecture. To quote again from *Notes and Elevations:* "It is also said that during the Genna era [1615–24] and in the early years of the Kan'ei era [1624–44], when the third shogun, Iemitsu, announced his visit, various daimyos prepared resplendent buildings to welcome him. Most of the residences had either an *omune* gate [a gate with two main pillars, two supporting pillars, and a gabled roof] or a two-story gate in front. There were a *genkan, tozamurai,* a *shikidai,* an *ohiroma* (with a *chumon,* a *kurumayose,* a *jodan,* a wooden-floored tokonoma, *chigaidana,* and *chodaigamae*), a *shoin* for the shogun, and a reception room. There were also rooms for the mistress of the house and for the servants, a large kitchen, and other buildings."

The *ohiroma* in the *shuden* style, which, as the document indicates, was formerly considered quite fashionable, was used less frequently in daimyo residences after the Tokugawa government became stabilized. From *Shomei* we know that the building style with a *kurumayose* and a *chumon* was used in the residences of the warriors living in Edo until the

1640s. These structures are mentioned in other documents that include descriptions of *ohiroma* in the residences of daimyos. From these documents we know that a *kurumayose* and a *chumon* were built in Councilor Owari's residence in Edo, in Sasayama Castle in Kyoto in 1609, and in the Hommaru Compound of Sendai Castle in 1610.

A document prepared by the Kora family about 1708 describes the residences in Edo during the late 1620s as follows: "The residence of Yorinori, the daimyo of Kii Province [present-day Wakayama Prefecture]—an *ohiroma* with a *chumon* and a *kurumayose*; all other structures are in accordance with tradition. The residence of Yorifusa, the daimyo of Hitachi Province [present-day Ibaraki Prefecture] —the *ohiroma, genkan, shikidai, tozamurai*, stables, and other structures do not differ from those used in Yorinori's residence. The residence of Matsudaira Tadamasa, daimyo of Echizen Province [present-day Fukui Prefecture]—the *ohiroma*, superior to the others in size, is commonly known as *senjojiki* [1,000-mat floor]; this *ohiroma* has a *chumon* and a *kurumayose*. All in all, the structures are of the same high quality as those of the *ohiroma* in the Hommaru Compound of Edo Castle. The residence of Matsudaira Mitsunobu, daimyo of Echigo Province [present-day Niigata Prefecture]—the *ohiroma* has a *chumon* and a *kurumayose*."

Although the *ohiroma* in the Hommaru Compound of Edo Castle was in the *shuden* style and had a *chumon* and a *kurumayose*, for some reason this style is no longer seen in daimyo residences after the Kan'ei era. As I mentioned earlier, this may be directly related to the stabilization of the Tokugawa government. Moreover, the *shuden* style disappears completely from daimyo residences built after the great Meireki fire.

SURVIVING SHOIN   Although many *shoin* structures on castle grounds were demolished under the reforms of the Meiji Restoration, and numerous others that had become public properties fell into ruin from lack of proper maintenance, we can still see fine *shoin* today. *Shoin* remaining at their original sites are the Kaitoku-kan in Kochi Castle, the Seison-kaku (Fig.

*140.* Chigaidana *and* tsukeshoin *in the 4.5-mat room, Dojinsai, in Togudo. 1485. Jisho-ji (Ginkaku-ji) temple, Kyoto.*

144) in Kenroku-en park in Kanazawa City, and the *shoin* found in the palace buildings in the Ninomaru Compound of Nijo Castle. Among the structures that are said to have been moved from their original sites are the guest hall of Kita-in (Fig. 80) in Saitama Prefecture (moved from Edo Castle), the guest hall in Kannon-ji temple in Shiga Prefecture (moved from Nagahara Palace), and the guest hall of Saikyo-ji temple (Fig. 145) in Shiga Prefecture (taken from Fushimi Castle). There are a number of *shoin* structures in the Kyoto area that are also said to have been moved from Fushimi Castle, but there is as yet no conclusive proof of such a transfer.

Most of the Imperial Palace study halls and the structures known as *tsune no goten* (private residential quarters of the emperor) survive today, in the residences of aristocrats, and these provide the best

141. Tokonoma and tsukeshoin *in living room of guest hall of Kangaku-in. 1600. Onjo-ji temple, Otsu, Shiga Prefecture. (See also Figures 77, 78, 142.)*

142. Guest hall of Kangaku-in. 1600. Onjo-ji temple, Otsu, Shiga Prefecture. (See also Figures 77, 78, 141.)

143. *Guest hall of Kanchi-in. 1605. To-ji temple, Kyoto.* *(See also Figure 89.)*

144. Jodan *in audience suite of Seison-kaku. 1863. Kanazawa, Ishikawa Prefecture.*

145. Chigaidana *and tokonoma in guest hall of Saikyo-ji temple. 1598. Sakamoto, Shiga Prefecture.*

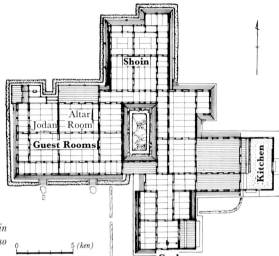

146. *Floor plan of monks' quarters, Kita-in, built in Saitama Prefecture in the seventeenth century. (See also Figures 79, 80.)*

0       5 *(ken)*

examples of the *shoin* style. Among the notable *shoin* structures transferred from the Imperial Palace are the *shinden* (Fig. 87) and *shoin* (Fig. 150) in Kanju-ji temple in Kyoto, the large *shoin* of Myoho-in temple in Kyoto, the guest hall (Figs. 82, 103) in the grounds of Shugaku-in Detached Palace in Kyoto, the *shinden* (Fig. 86) of Emman-in in the Onjo-ji temple complex in Shiga Prefecture, and the *hojo,* or abbot's quarters (Fig. 108), of Honen-in temple in Kyoto. Of *shoin* built in temples, there are the audience suite (Fig. 97) and the *shiroshoin* (Fig. 96) of Nishi Hongan-ji in Kyoto; the *hojo* (Fig. 139) of Konchi-in, a subtemple of Nanzen-ji in Kyoto; and the large and small *hojo* (Figs. 105, 153) in Chion-in in Kyoto.

Aside from these formal reception rooms in the *shoin* style from the residences of warriors, aristocrats, and priests, there are some *shoin* surviving from the Edo period that were built in the *sukiya* (tearoom) style of architecture and that have a relaxed atmosphere. The most famous buildings in this style are those in the Katsura Detached Palace in Kyoto. Others include Jugetsu-kan in the Shu-gaku-in Detached Palace grounds in Kyoto; Rin-shun-kaku (Figs. 126, 157, 158) in Sankei-en park in Yokohama; the *kuroshoin* (Fig. 127) in the Nishi Hongan-ji temple in Kyoto; the large and small *shoin* (Figs. 128, 129) in Manshu-in temple in Kyoto; and the *shoin* (Fig. 132) in Jiko-in temple in Nara. Most of these existing structures in the *shoin* style were built in Buddhist temples for superiors to receive guests in or for use as their own quarters.

Dojinsai (Fig. 140) is a four-and-a-half-mat room containing a *tsukeshoin* and *chigaidana* and is located in the northeastern section of the Togudo in the Jisho-ji temple grounds in Kyoto. It was formerly the private Buddhist chapel of the Ashikaga shogun Yoshimasa (1434–90). Jisho-ji, usually called Gin-kaku-ji, or Silver Pavilion, was a pavilion of Yoshimasa's villa and was converted into a Buddhist temple after his death. The *Onryoken Diary* (the official diary of Shokoku-ji temple in Kyoto, in which various events of Yoshimasa's time are recorded) mentions that Dojinsai was used as a study and for holding tea ceremonies and that its *chigaidana* were decorated with books and other objects.

Dojinsai is the oldest *shoin* structure in existence today.

The Kojo-in and Kangaku-in guest halls, located in the grounds of Onjo-ji temple near Lake Biwa in Shiga Prefecture, were the most important buildings in the temple complex and were used for residential and reception purposes. The main room of the audience suite (Figs. 78, 142) in the Kangaku-in guest hall is adorned with a tokonoma, and the living room (Fig. 141) located next to it has a tokonoma and a *tsukeshoin*.

In the guest hall of Kanchi-in (Fig. 143), a subtemple located in the grounds of To-ji in Kyoto, the rooms have different combinations of room decorations: the main room (Fig. 89) has a tokonoma and *chigaidana*, and the living room has a *tsukeshoin* and *chodaigamae* (the doors in this case are not merely decorative but serve as an entrance to the adjoining *chodai*). The Kangaku-in and the Kanchi-in guest halls both have a *chumon* and a *kurumayose* with a *karahafu* gable (Figs. 142, 143), as do the Kojo-in guest hall (Fig. 76) and the *shoin* (Fig. 102) in Sambo-in, a subtemple of Daigo-ji temple in Kyoto. But in the latter two, the living quarters were eliminated and only the rooms for holding formal receptions remained. In Kojo-in, the *jodan* of the main room projects onto the veranda, and there are *chodaigamae* as additional adornments.

In 1836 the daimyo Maeda Nariyasu built Seison-kaku, a residence for his mother's retirement. Of the buildings of Seison-kaku, the audience room (Fig. 144), tearoom, and sleeping room survive today in Ishikawa Prefecture. Because this palace complex was intended for a retired lady and was built at the end of the Edo period, it does not have the commanding air of the palaces in the Nijo Castle grounds. The audience room, for example, while equipped with all four formal room decorations—tokonoma, *chigaidana*, *tsukeshoin*, and *chodaigamae*—still has a relaxed atmosphere. There are attempts to use new materials, such as glass, on the second floor and in other parts of this building.

The plate nailed to the ridgepole of the guest hall (Fig. 145) in the Saikyo-ji temple grounds, Shiga Prefecture, records that the hall was built in

147. *Tokonoma and* chigaidana *in* shoin *of Kannon-ji temple. Seventeenth century. Kusatsu, Shiga Prefecture.*

1598 at the wish of the wife of Tachibana Nagaharu, who was a vassal of Toyotomi Hideyoshi. However, the claim that the guest hall was constructed of materials from the palace complex of Fushimi Castle is considered credible because of the spacing of the outer columns at intervals of one *ken* (1.97 meters) and because of the numerous repair marks on the *tenjo nageshi, uchinori nageshi,* and lintels. The materials were probably taken from Fushimi Castle after it collapsed in the earthquake of 1596.

The guest hall (Figs. 80, 146) of Kita-in temple in Saitama Prefecture is called the "hall where Iemitsu was born" by those connected with the temple. Iemitsu, the third Tokugawa shogun, presented a building from the Edo Castle grounds to the temple during the rebuilding of Kita-in in 1638, and its guest hall, *shoin,* and kitchen were

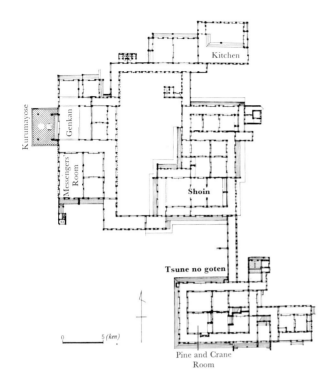

*148. Floor plan of Hommaru Palace constructed in 1847 and moved to Nijo Castle in Kyoto in 1894.*

built from this material. The *shoin* probably came from the women's quarters and was reconstructed in its present style when it was moved, although some think it came from the palace built for Lady Kasuga, Iemitsu's wet nurse.

In the plans of Edo Castle, drawn in 1640 and owned by Yoshihide Okuma, the floor plan that most resembles that of the Kita-in guest hall is that of Lady Kasuga's palace. It is possible, then, that the guest hall, not the *shoin*, was built of materials from this palace. The guest hall of Kita-in has a *jodan* (Fig. 80) equipped with a tokonoma and *chigaidana*, and its ceiling (Fig. 79), painted in brilliant colors, is decorated with metalwork embossed with the Tokugawa family crest. Originally the guest hall had four rooms, but when the present hall was built, two more rooms were added in order to place the altar room at the center of the building.

*149.* Chigaidana *and tokonoma in Pine and Crane room of* tsune no goten *of Hommaru Palace of Nijo Castle. 1847; moved to present site 1894. Kyoto. (See also Figure 148.)*

*150.* Shoin *of Kanju-ji temple. Moved to present site 1684–88. Kyoto.*

*151.* Fusuma *paper decorated with chrysanthemum pattern, from* shinden *of Kanju-ji temple. 1676. Kyoto. (See also Figure 87.)*

*152. L-shaped* jodan, tokonoma *(with arched window),* chigaidana, *and* chodaigamae *in* hondo *of Zuigan-ji temple. 1609. Matsushima, Miyagi Prefecture.*

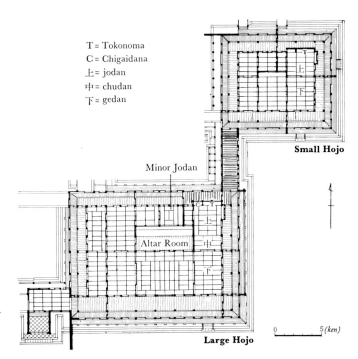

T = Tokonoma
C = Chigaidana
上 = jodan
中 = chudan
下 = gedan

Small Hojo

Minor Jodan

Altar Room

Large Hojo

0 — 5 (ken)

*153. Floor plans of large and small* hojo *of Chion-in, built in Kyoto in 1641. (See also Figure 105.)*

The materials for the *shoin* (Fig. 147) of Kannon-ji temple in Shiga Prefecture were said to have been given to the temple from Nagahara Palace, where the shoguns stayed on their journeys to Kyoto, when it was dismantled in 1685. During recent repair work a plate used when offering incense and prayers was discovered. Dedicated to the Eleven-headed Kannon, the plate bears the date 1559. This would seem a strong indication that the *shoin* was constructed earlier than 1685; however, since some documents clearly show that Ashiura Kannon-ji was in charge of the construction of Nagahara Palace in 1634, the possibility that the *shoin* did come from the palace cannot be entirely ruled out. Nonetheless, some of the carpentry techniques are old enough to support the temple's claim that this building was constructed in 1559.

The buildings of the present Imperial Residence of the Kyoto Imperial Palace were rebuilt in 1855 to replace the ones that burned down in 1854. At that time Shishin-den and Seiryo-den (Figs. 66, 67), the principal buildings in the complex, were used for ceremonies. These structures inherited the style of palace architecture traditionally followed since the late thirteenth century. The newer *shoin* style, better suited for audience purposes, was adopted in the *tsune no goten* (Fig. 110), the *gakumonjo* (literally, "study hall"; Fig. 107), and the *kogosho* (the palace for the crown prince). These *shoin*-style buildings used by the court aristocrats are not as elaborately decorated as the *shoin* in the Ninomaru Palace of the Nijo Castle complex, which are representative of the *shoin* of the warriors.

During the years between 1621 and 1624 a palace in the Hommaru Compound of Nijo Castle was built to receive the Tokugawa shogun Hidetada; however, this palace was destroyed in a fire in 1788. When Nijo Castle became one of the imperial villas after the Meiji Restoration, the palace (Fig. 148) of the last member of the Katsura family—

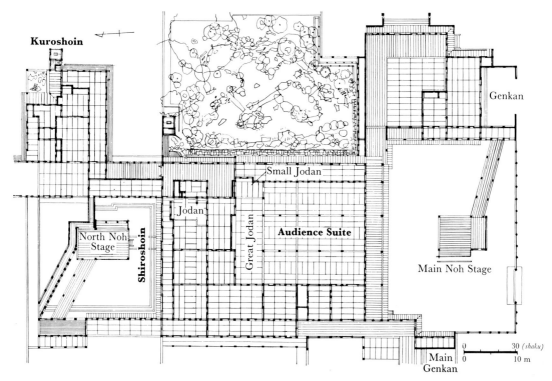

**Kuroshoin**

Genkan

Small Jodan

Jodan

Great Jodan

**Audience Suite**

North Noh Stage

**Shiroshoin**

Main Noh Stage

0 — 30 (shaku)
0 — 10 m

Main Genkan

*154. Floor plan of Nishi Hongan-ji temple in Kyoto.*

including the *tsune no goten* (Fig. 149), the middle *shoin*, the audience suite, and the *kurumayose*—was transferred in 1894 from its location north of the Imperial Palace to the Nijo Castle grounds. The three-story *tsune no goten* has a quiet atmosphere in a *sukiya* style of architecture; the middle *shoin* has an audience suite with a fourteen-mat *jodan*. These rare and important buildings tell us much about the architectural styles used by aristocrats during the late Edo period.

In 1619 a palace was built for the daughter of the Tokugawa shogun Hidetada when she joined the court of Emperor Gomizuno-o. When the palace was dismantled in 1641, the *otsubone* (ladies' quarters) was given to Emman-in temple in Shiga Prefecture; and it was from this material that the *shinden* (Figs. 86, 109) of Emman-in was built in 1647. The floor plan of the new building was substantially different from that of the *otsubone,* but it

succeeded in retaining the atmosphere of the former structure because its tokonoma, *chigaidana*, and *chodaigamae* were arranged in accordance with the original plans.

The Shugaku-in Detached Palace, a villa built in Kyoto during the Jo-o era (1652–55) and designed by Emperor Gomizuno-o himself, still remains in its original state. The guest hall of the middle garden (Figs. 82, 103) of the palace grounds, designed in 1677 for Hidetada's daughter Kazuko, was used as the palace audience hall. After Hidetada's daughter died in 1678, the guest hall was given to Rinkyu-ji temple (in 1682) and used there as a guest hall. The veranda is close to the ground because the columns of the building were shortened in the process of moving in order to set the building on stonework. The middle garden, including the guest hall, became part of the detached palace when it was given to the imperial family by the

155. *Small* jodan *viewed from great* jodan *in audience suite of Nishi Hongan-ji temple. Seventeenth century. Kyoto. (See also Figures 93, 97, 154.)*

temple in 1868. The interior design is tasteful and the *chigaidana* are particularly noteworthy. The walls of the tokonoma and *chigaidana* are decorated with cards bearing poems instead of with a painting as we have seen in other structures.

The *shoin* (Fig. 150) of Kanju-ji temple in Kyoto was transferred to the temple in 1684–88. Temple history records that its *shoin* came from the palace of the retired emperor Gosai, but it is not known from which of the palace buildings. However, we know more about the *shinden*, which was transferred to the temple in 1697. Before it was moved to Kanju-ji, the *shinden* was the audience hall of Myosho-in Palace, built in 1676 for the former empress Myosho, who was the daughter of Gomizuno-o and Tofukumon-in (Tokugawa Kazuko).

Externally, the *shinden* retains the old aristocratic style, with a staircase canopy, or porch roof, at-tached to the middle of the building; inside there is a *jodan* adorned with a tokonoma, *chigaidana*, and a *tsukeshoin*. Among the important differences between the original building and the form it took after it was moved are that the original roofing of cypress bark was replaced with curved tiles; alterations were made in the floor so that it would adjust to the ground formation; new *chigaidana* were put up and the old shelves were placed in the *shoin*; and the paper with a design of chrysanthemums (the imperial crest) scattered on a checkered pattern (Fig. 151), used on the walls and *fusuma*, was replaced with plain white paper. A building similar to this *shinden* is the *shinden* of Ichijo-in temple, moved to the Toshodai-ji temple grounds in Nara.

The *hojo* of Honen-in temple in Kyoto was transferred there in 1680. This *shoin* building was originally built in 1675 in Kyoto for Emperor

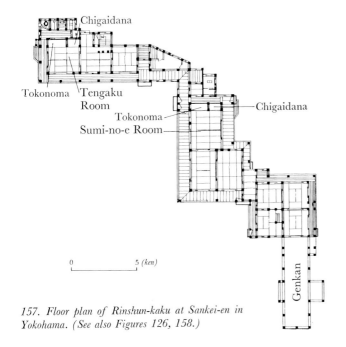

Chigaidana

Tokonoma   Tengaku Room

Tokonoma

Sumi-no-e Room

Chigaidana

0        5 (ken)

Genkan

*157. Floor plan of Rinshun-kaku at Sankei-en in Yokohama. (See also Figures 126, 158.)*

*158. Rinshun-kaku. 1649; moved to present site 1915. Sankei-en, Yokohama. (See also Figures 126, 157.)*

Gosai's daughter Yao, and its overall design has an atmosphere of calmness appropriate for a princess. The main room's inner wall (Fig. 108), almost four meters wide, is divided in half, with half the space for a tokonoma and the other half for *chigaidana*. The pictures of paulownia painted on the walls of these two decorative elements and the paintings on the *fusuma* adjoining them form a series, and bear the marks of the move. The designs on the screens, which were made from the old *fusuma*, are Japanese pine. These paintings are attributed to Kano Mitsunobu (1561–1608), one of Tan'yu's uncles, but there is no conclusive proof to support this attribution. If the paintings were originally painted for the *shoin*, those of Japanese pine could not have been done by Mitsunobu, who died long before the *shoin* was built, but must have been executed by one of the four painters—Eishin, Dosetsu, Ukyo, or Takumi—who were responsible for decorating the *fusuma* in Gosai's palace.

Both the *hojo* (Fig. 139) in the Konchi-in sub-temple of Nanzen-ji in Kyoto and the *hondo* (Fig. 152) in Zuigan-ji temple, Miyagi Prefecture, are altar rooms and audience suites for the abbots. They are outstanding among the many *hojo* in existence, and in each of them the Buddhist altar room is in the center of the building. Adjoining the altar room there is also a room with a *jodan* adorned with a tokonoma, *chigaidana*, and a *tsukeshoin*. In Konchi-in, the *chodaigamae* installed for the shogun's use at receptions project considerably into the room because of the adjoining altar room. The Zuigan-ji *hojo* was used for receiving daimyos visiting local officials; and its *fusuma* have paintings by artists of the Kano school. In Zuigan-ji there is the frame of an arched window called a *katomado* in the middle of the tokonoma wall, and *fusuma* replace the usual *chodaigamae*. How the *katomado* was used remains unknown. Since the outermost sections of the *hojo* were customarily used as one large room, the three

◁ *156. View from L-shaped jodan in main room of* shiroshoin *of Nishi Hongan-ji temple. Seventeenth century. Kyoto. (See also Figures 96, 98, 154.)*

159. Tsukeshoin, *tokonoma, and* chigaidana *in Brocade Room of the Sumiya. C. 1787. Kyoto.*

160 (*opposite page, left*). *Tokonoma and* ▷ tsukeshoin *in* shoin *of Yoshimura residence. Seventeenth century. Habikino, Osaka.*

161 (*opposite page, right*). *Tokonoma and* ▷ chigaidana *in* shoin *of the Sasagawa residence. 1826. Ajikata, Niigata Prefecture.*

rooms were separated by removable *fusuma*. In order to hold audiences it was necessary to build a *jodan*, which is L-shaped in this case, within the inner room.

The large and small *hojo* shown in Figures 105 and 153 are located in the Chion-in temple grounds in Kyoto. Chion-in is the head temple of the Jodo sect; and the Tokugawas, traditionally members of this sect, had a longstanding relationship with the temple. For the renovation of the temple during the second quarter of the seventeenth century, the third shogun, Iemitsu, appointed Katagiri Sekishu (1603–73) superintendent and placed the Nakai family in charge; the large and small *hojo* survive from this renovation. The large *hojo* was used for audiences and religious rites and ceremonies, whereas the small *hojo* (Fig. 105) was equivalent to the *gozanoma* of a warrior's residence.

The audience suite (Figs. 93, 97, 155) and the *shiroshoin* (Figs. 96, 98, 156) of Nishi Hongan-ji temple are both currently used for formal functions. The *fusuma* and walls of both are beautifully decorated with designs on a gold ground. The audience

suite, called the Stork Room, is used by the abbot for holding formal receptions. It was long believed that the Stork Room was the audience suite of Hideyoshi's Fushimi Castle and that the room had been moved from the castle as a gift to the temple. As a result of recent repair work, however, the Stork Room appears to have been originally built in the temple grounds during the years 1624–44. The transfer of the building could not have been possible, since the principal buildings of Fushimi Castle had already been destroyed once by earthquake and once by fire before this period of construction.

The Stork Room (Konoma) is so named because of the storks carved in the *ramma*—the openwork transom just below the *kokabe* between the *jodan* and the *gedan* (Figs. 97, 155). On the floor directly below the *ramma* is a thick, lacquered sill that clearly separates the *jodan* and the *gedan*. According to the theory of Michio Fujioka, a professor of architectural history, the *jodan*, with its window shaped like the ceremonial fan used by a military commander, was set up as part of the preparations made to

receive the third Tokugawa shogun, Iemitsu, whose visit never materialized. The *jodan* runs the entire width of the room except for one section raised an additional step (Fig. 155), where one supposes Iemitsu would have sat. During receptions the abbot sits in the middle of the *jodan,* before the tokonoma, which is almost six meters wide. On his left and right sit his son (heir) and brothers.

The court noble Kujo, who was the adoptive father of the abbot, was received in the *shiroshoin,* and on that occasion the dressing room adjoining the *shoin* was used for changing costume. There are two Noh stages in the courtyard, one facing the audience suite and one facing the *shiroshoin;* they were relocated and rebuilt from old stages that had long been in the two buildings. Stagings of Noh plays in these buildings are recorded in the *Ishiyama Hongan-ji Diary.* The *kuroshoin* (Fig. 127), connected by roofed corridors to the audience suite (Fig. 154), is used as the abbot's private quarters. In contrast to the audience suite, which has a lavishly decorated interior, the design of the *kuroshoin* is very informal and refreshing in its simplicity. The design

of the tokonoma, *chigaidana, tsukeshoin,* some of the pillars, and so on shows the influence of *sukiya* architecture.

The *shoin* (Fig. 138) of Katsura Detached Palace in Kyoto was built in the years 1615–25 and was expanded around 1645. The palace, at first the villa built around 1620 by Prince Toshihito, Emperor Goyozei's brother, consisted mainly of this *shoin.* Its expansion was begun by Prince Noritada in 1642 and continued until 1658, the year the retired emperor Gomizuno-o visited. This *shoin,* in the *sukiya* style of architecture, and the other buildings built to harmonize with the extraordinary garden are well known.

Rinshun-kaku (Figs. 157, 158) was transferred in 1915 to the Sankei-en park, Yokohama. It was originally built on the Kinokawa river in 1649 as the villa of the daimyo of Kii Province. As in Katsura Detached Palace, the *sukiya* style of architecture was employed. The various beams and pillars are of polished logs, and we find a simplified version of the formal *tsukeshoin.* An informal treatment in design lends a relaxed air to the whole structure. *Shoin* in the *sukiya* style of architecture seem to have been widely used by the warriors, as well as by the aristocrats, in their villas, since formal audiences were not held there. Among the other distinguished examples of *shoin* in this style are the Jugetsu-kan, one of the main buildings located in the lower garden of the Shugaku-in Detached Palace grounds; Choshu-kaku, a pavilion said to have been transferred from Nijo Castle to the Sankei-en grounds; and Hiun-kaku, a pavilion located in the Nishi Hongan-ji temple grounds.

Manshu-in, a temple in Kyoto, was moved to its present site in 1656. Its large and small *shoin* (Figs. 128, 129) were built in 1656 by Prince Ryosho, who had become a priest. Ryosho was the second son of Prince Toshihito, the owner of Katsura Detached Palace. The temple gave away its *shinden* during the Meiji era; but most of the other buildings survive in the temple grounds, including the large *shoin*, which was originally used solely for reception purposes, and the small *shoin*, the living quarters of the prince. Both the large and small *shoin* are simply designed, and the walls, finished in reds made from iron oxide, create a pleasant contrast with the white *shoji*. The plan of the large *shoin* is typical of *shoin* in a temple whose abbot is from the imperial family. In the large *shoin* there are two rooms, each of which has a tokonoma. The main room of the small *shoin* is similar to the *jodan* in the *shoin* in Katsura Detached Palace in regard to the elaborate *chigaidana* and the *ramma* with chrysanthemum crests.

Among the distinguished *shoin* structures owned by private individuals are the Sumiya (Fig. 159) in Kyoto, and those owned by the Yoshimuras in Osaka (Fig. 160), the Watanabes in Niigata Prefecture (Figs. 130, 131), and the Sasagawas in Niigata Prefecture (Fig. 161). The walls in the *shoin* of the Watanabe family are covered with paper decorated with cedar designs, and the walls in the *shoin* of the Sasagawa family have designs of cranes in gold and silver. The use of woodblock-printed paper to decorate interiors became fashionable in the late eighteenth century, regardless of class; this type of decoration may have become popular because commoners had been forbidden to paint walls and *fusuma*. After the murals done in heavy, brilliant colors, the printed paper appears totally fresh.

Sumiya (Fig. 159), formerly one of the best-known pleasure houses in the Shimabara entertainment district of Kyoto, was built in 1640 and expanded in 1787. The plans, originally those for a commoner's house, were changed extensively as the building was expanded. Because of the type of business conducted there, the building was frequently renovated, and each room had a totally different interior. The main rooms have a tokonoma and *chigaidana*, but the usual *shoin* style employed was boldly altered. The designs on the *shoji*, the *fusuma*, and the ceilings are among the most elaborate and unusual ever used.

Unfortunately, little attention has been given to the architecture of the Edo period. This was a time when the daimyos built up a ruling system and a hierarchy distinct from those of the medieval period. And architecturally, interest in the shrine and the temple, the principal structures up until then, was replaced by interest in structures characteristic of the warrior—castles and *shoin*—which were built as symbols of status and power. The warriors were the ruling class during the Edo period, and their castles and *shoin* played an integral part in their efforts to express and maintain the status they had gained. In this sense these structures, standing in the foreground of Edo architecture, tell us almost as much about the shifting balance of power as they do about changing tastes and architectural techniques.

# TITLES IN THE SERIES

Although the individual books in the series are designed as self-contained units, so that readers may choose subjects according to their personal interests, the series itself constitutes a full survey of Japanese art and is therefore a reference work of great value. The following titles are listed in the same order, roughly chronological, as those of the original Japanese versions, with the addition of a cultural appreciation (Vol. 30) and the index volume.

The "weathermark" identifies this book as having been planned, designed, and produced at the Tokyo offices of John Weatherhill, Inc., 7-6-13 Roppongi, Minato-ku, Tokyo 106. Book design and typography by Meredith Weatherby and Ronald V. Bell. Layout of photographs by Rebecca Davis. Composition by General Printing Co., Yokohama. Color plates engraved and printed by Nissha Printing Co., Kyoto. Gravure plates engraved and printed by Inshokan Printing Co., Tokyo. Monochrome letterpress platemaking and printing and text printing by Toyo Printing Co., Tokyo. Bound at the Makoto Binderies, Tokyo. Text is set in 10-pt. Monotype Baskerville with hand-set Optima for display.

A000015929037